Beauty
In Battle

Beauty
In Battle

WINNING IN MARRIAGE
BY WAGING A WAR

Jason & Tori Benham

This book is dedicated to our kids—
Trae, Allie, Jake, and Lundi.
You have taught us more than you'll ever know.
Thank you for your patience.
We love you with all our hearts.

ACKNOWLEDGMENTS

This book is a dream come true for us. Ever since our dating years, we've talked about being involved in helping to strengthen marriages and what that might look like. Of course, no marriage is a breeze. (That's what this book is about, after all!) We had to get our butts kicked for a little while, but ultimately, we've been able to move toward that dream together. But we couldn't do it alone.

We thank the Lord for His continued guidance as we worked through the writing process and His faithfulness in empowering us to love and appreciate each other through it. We thank our respective parents for modeling faithfulness in marriage, showing us the value of relationship, and standing in our corner and believing in us.

Specifically, we want to thank our amazing team of editors.

Karla Dial, our chief editor and coach—your talents are truly a gift. We're better writers and people, having worked with you. Honestly, you were a dream.

Bonita Jewel—working through each chapter with you was a joy. Won't write another book without you!

Patrick Conley—not only are you one of the best preachers we've heard, you are a ninja-assassin wordsmith with enough fight and grit to take down an army. You're a valuable weapon in any writer's arsenal.

Lastly, we want to thank Emerson and Sarah Eggerichs. Your book *Love & Respect* not only rocked our worlds and gave us a simple way to understand each other, but it provided a theological foundation upon which we've formulated many of the thoughts in this book. While Emerson's name is on the cover, we know Sarah is the real genius behind its success! Thank you for your friendship and the way you've personally poured into us. Our time spent with you has made us better. We love you.

CONTENTS

SOMEBODY CALL 911

"Sorry to bug you, Jason," our front desk attendant said as she popped her head into my office early that Tuesday morning, "but you need to pray. A plane just flew into one of the World Trade Center buildings in New York City."

Sometimes in life, people remember exactly where they were when something happened. Tori and I grew up hearing where people were when JFK was shot, when Neil Armstrong walked on the moon, and when Martin Luther King Jr. was assassinated. While those events were before our time, we remember in vivid detail everything surrounding that fateful day on September 11, 2001, when nineteen terrorists brought our nation to its knees.

We had just moved to Charlotte, North Carolina, and had been married all of nine months. Tori was four months pregnant and working as a nanny. I was a corporate chaplain at a large company.

I threw up a quick prayer for the people involved, but before I could even say, "Amen," another coworker burst through the door.

"A second plane just hit the other World Trade Center building!" he called as he ran through the hall. "And it was a big one!"

I jumped out of my chair and followed him to the

conference room. A small group of employees had already gathered around a television. I couldn't believe what I was seeing. Clouds of black smoke billowed out of the two tallest buildings in New York City. Eyewitnesses spoke of seeing two commercial airline jets fly into the buildings just minutes apart. A short time later, another plane crashed into the Pentagon, and then we heard about a fourth crashing down in a field in Pennsylvania.

Every television station we turned to was filled with dreadful images. Screaming people ran through the streets of New York as a hellish cloud of smoke and ash drove them down the city blocks. Some staggered along in shock. Some had makeshift bandages wrapped around their heads or limbs. Others didn't seem to notice they were injured as they stumbled along.

I left the office, hopped in my car, and sped home to be with Tori, who was glued to the television watching the news. In the moments that followed, we watched in horror as the Twin Towers fell to the ground.

When it was all said and done, 2,996 people died and more than six thousand were injured. It would go down as the deadliest terrorist strike in American history.

But it isn't just the sight of the planes crashing into the buildings or the people jumping to their deaths in desperate attempts to survive that are etched in our memory forever; it was the lesson on relationships we learned in the weeks and months that followed. We felt an overwhelming camaraderie and brotherly love toward total strangers and experienced a bond with people we'd never even met. We found ourselves united with people from all walks of life with whom we had nothing in common except the fact that we were Americans, and we were in a fight.

As life slowly resumed, professional sports teams locked arms with their opponents before games, emergency personnel received standing ovations everywhere they went, complete strangers talked to each other as if they were lifelong friends, and politicians stopped arguing and started collaborating. A collective sense of unity pervaded our nation like never before.

As strange as it sounds, it was a good time to be an American. We all dropped our differences and saw each other not as Republicans or Democrats, white or black, rich or poor, Christian or atheist—we saw ourselves as brothers and sisters. And for that brief moment in history, we were united.

What had changed? How did this pervasive unity miraculously appear? It wasn't because we all read the same book on getting along and decided to apply its principles.

What brought us together was the fact that we were in a fight. And we knew we *had* to stay together.

We had a common enemy and a common goal. Our enemy wasn't *in here* but *out there*. We knew that—despite our superficial differences—we weren't enemies. We understood that we needed to stop fighting *against* each other and start fighting *alongside* one another against our true enemy—one who wanted nothing more than to take us out.

In the process, we discovered that *fighting together drew us together*.

Tori:

Living through the tragedy of 9-11 in our first year of marriage gave us a powerful picture of how to remain united despite our differences. We saw firsthand how strength comes through strain, and how the fight that was meant to tear people apart can actually draw them together. We have discovered in our own relationship that beauty results when we choose to no longer fight *against* each other in a personal battle but *alongside* one another in a spiritual war.

The problem that so often happens in marriage is that we fight the wrong battle. We wage war against each other rather than the real enemy—Satan. Many of us are not even aware of his desire to take us down. So, we end up as adversaries rather than allies. Somehow, we buy the lie that we are enemies—while the real enemy wreaks havoc on our sacred relationship.

We know what this feels like. In our first year of marriage, Jason and I discovered what many young couples do—the things we once liked about each other didn't seem so likeable anymore. And in the years that followed, we only experienced more of the same. Arguments and fights became commonplace. Little did we know, that was the plan of the enemy all along: to get us fighting face-to-face against each other rather than shoulder-to-shoulder against him. This approach kept us returning to the same relational rut over and over.

But then God woke us up! He *literally* woke Jason up—like, an out-of-a-sound-sleep-in-the-middle-of-the-night type of thing. We'll tell you more about that later, but this wake-up call changed the trajectory of our relationship. It put us on a path to discover how to use our struggles to increase the strength of our marriage—how to turn the fight into something that drew us together rather than something that tore us apart, just like what happened in our nation on 9-11.

We learned that we didn't need to *stop* fighting; we needed to *start* fighting ... the right way. That's why we wrote this book. We want to show you how fighting properly changed our marriage for the better, and how it can help you as well.

Jason:

Here's the crazy part: God created marriage to succeed in the context of a fight. It was in the earliest design. When He created the very first couple, Adam and Eve, He put them in the exact same place where He banished Satan—planet earth. The first wedding ceremony in human history was conducted within the context of a spiritual war.

Until you recognize you were made for a battle, you will never experience the full depth of relational intimacy for which God has created you. It isn't a physical fight, but a spiritual one. As you learn to fight it together, you'll discover that waging war in the spiritual will draw you together in the natural.

Many couples need to wake up to the real battle. The only way to discover the beauty *in* your marriage is to first be willing to enter the battle *for* your marriage. Maybe you and your spouse have not yet learned how you can experience power and unity by waging war this way. But as you walk through these pages with us, we'll show you how we did it. We'll give you the practical steps we took to turn conflict and quarrels into passion and purpose.

We'll take you to a basketball court where a flirtatious stranger exposed a problem in our relationship. You'll travel along with us on a cruise ship where a suitcase was flung across our room. We'll invite you to a party where one of us (not mentioning names!) jumped across a kitchen island to punch someone in the face. We'll even walk you into our master bedroom, where God used a dream to reignite our passion for each other, and the three-step plan He gave us to get it back.

Weaved into these stories, here are some foundational truths we want you to see:

- You have a very real enemy who hates you and your marriage.
- His goal is to get you to fight alongside him against your spouse.
- God has designed you to fight alongside your spouse against him.
- Fighting together draws you together.
- The fight that once separated you can be used to strengthen you.

We will dive deeper into each of these truths as we share our story and a few of the stories from couples we've counseled over the years. We'll share with you how insecurity from the past can creep into your present and rob you of your power. We'll talk about conflict and the two things that always manifest themselves when issues arise. We'll discuss the importance of thinking properly toward your spouse and three steps to counteract negative thoughts. And we'll show you how dreaming about what you *could* be as a couple will help you achieve what *should* be in your marriage.

At the end of each chapter, we've written a few questions for you and your spouse to discuss together. They were designed to spark deep conversations that will strengthen your relationship if you let them. Please, take the time to talk through each of them before you move on to the next chapter. (And if your husband doesn't want to discuss them with you, ladies, tell him I'm gonna smack him!)

Joking aside, I know it's not easy. The joy of your marriage journey may be a distant memory as you hold this book in your hand, praying and hoping that God will reignite that old relational flame once again. His promise to you is that He can … and He *will*. He did it for us and He'll do it for you. Even better, He *wants* to—if you'll let Him. Hold onto God's promises and don't lose hope. Cling to Him in faith and let Him breathe new life into your relationship.

Wherever you are in your marriage journey, the stories and principles we're going to share with you will help you in your relationship. The most important lessons we've learned in marriage are documented in these pages. We can't wait to dive in and show you how we found beauty in the midst of battle.

To kick things off, let us take you to one of our favorite little spots—a place where love is hate and hate is love. The sign above the door says it all, really.

CHAPTER 1

TWO WODS IN ONE DAY

"Out of suffering have emerged the strongest of souls."
– Khalil Gibran

Tori:

"I Hate You. I Hate This Place. See You Tomorrow."

Those words are on a sign hanging over the exit of the gym where we work out. If you are at all familiar with CrossFit, you know how appropriate it is.

If you know nothing about CrossFit, it is basically a bunch of people who come together to lift heavy things, strain every fiber of their beings, and sweat profusely—all while vowing to never come back. Then, we show up the next day and do it all over again.

It is highly addictive, and its fans are so intensely dedicated that some have labeled it "cult-fit." It's amazing how a little competition, along with the community aspect of the workouts, keeps people coming back and begging for more.

CrossFit's success proves that those who suffer together stay together. Kind of like marriage.

Over a decade ago, before Jason and I encountered Cross-Fit, I thought my competitive juices had long run dry. Sure, Jason loved competition, but boys take longer to mature, right? I was past that—or so I thought.

I was weeks away from giving birth to our fourth child when Jason got his first taste of the CrossFit Kool-Aid. A buddy showed him a video of all these crazy people flipping tires, carrying sandbags on their shoulders, doing pushups and pullups, and running up hills in a group workout. He got so excited to try it he woke up at 5 the next morning and joined the nearest "box" (a gym dedicated to CrossFit). Then he spent the next few weeks begging me to do the same.

Fast forward a month or so. Our fourth baby had been born, and with nursing pads ever so near, I took my first sip of the CrossFit juice. Then, a gulp. Then I guzzled the whole darn thing. I was hooked.

Come to find out, my competitive drive had not gone missing. It had only been kept dormant by forty months of pregnancy. And it was back!

Of all the days we voluntarily punish ourselves at the gym, Saturdays are our favorite. Saturday is Team WOD. For those of you who don't speak CrossFit, WOD stands for "workout of the day." And the "team" part means just that: you compete as a team.

The coach chooses the teams—but every Saturday, I find myself hoping I'm with Jason. I love being on my husband's team for several reasons, but one of the main reasons (I will not say how high on the list!) is the fact that Jason knows how to win. He just has this way of overcoming the task in front of him. Everyone who knows him would agree he has a knack for making things happen.

Over the years, we have engaged in some epic team battles... but one particular Saturday stands out. It began with our coach calling out teams of two. I tried not to smile too much when I heard: "Jason and Tori."

WOD #1

Everyone gathered around as our coach wrote up the workout on the white board. Forty or so people were there, all of them ready to get started. Jason and I immediately started strategizing how to win.

This workout was to be done "You go-I go" style, where a given number of reps at each exercise station must be completed before moving on to the next. But only one teammate can work-out at a time. This is where the strategy becomes important; you want each team member working where they are strongest.

"Knock out as many pull-ups and jump ropes as you can," Jason said. He stood in front of me, eyeing the whiteboard. "I'm going to have to do most of the push-ups and the air bike."

Nodding in agreement, I stood with my hands on my hips, relieved he was on my team. His heavier body can generate twice as much power on the bike as mine can. The idea of him doing most of that was a good one! We continued to plan, trying to picture the best path to victory.

All around the room, other teams were doing the same. Then we heard the words all CrossFitters love to hate.

"Starting in ten!" the coach announced, beginning the countdown. (It is never long enough for what lies ahead.)

"... three, two, one, GO!"

Jason went first, as he always does in this style of workout. Before long, I could hear him hollering across the gym that he was almost done. I waited at the pull-up station while he finished his push-ups. As he knocked out the last few reps, he gave me a look that said, *You better be ready.*

As soon as he finished, I grabbed the pull-up bar and jumped into action. Halfway through my reps, I caught a glimpse of Jason striding briskly toward me.

"Get to the jump ropes!" he barked from a few feet away. "I'm going to knock out the rest of these."

"No!" I yelled back. I knew I had at least ten more reps in me. "I've got these!"

"STOP!" he yelled even louder as he bent over, hands on his knees. Drops of sweat marked the black rubber floor beneath him. "Just go do them."

Fifty reps into the jump rope, I realized why Jason had been so adamant about me quitting the pull-ups. My arms were completely exhausted. I thought I was going to die. Seeing me struggling, Jason ran over to help, but I knew the dreaded air bike was next.

"I got these!" I yelled. "Get to the bike!" As much as the jump rope station had become a world of agony, I knew Jason was much better on the bike than I was. And since I wanted to win, I picked my poison and endured the pain.

My shoulders and arms throbbed and my eyes stung from sweat as I completed my last rep. Jason was already in position on the air bike. The moment I dropped the rope, he started pedaling... furiously.

As I tried to catch my breath and calm my racing heart, I headed toward him. I hunched over near the bike, gathering my energy for the next set. *Don't normal moms have something better to do on a Saturday morning?* I thought. *I should still be in my bathrobe right now.*

"What are you doing?" Jason's voice snapped me back to attention. He was barely able to breathe, but he had enough wind to growl, "Get back to the push-ups."

One glance at the scowl on his red, sweaty face told me his mood matched his tone. Without a second thought, I rushed to the push-up station, where I waited with my ear tuned for Jason's "GO!"

I quickly surveyed the room to see how the other teams were doing. We were in first place, but one team was closing in quickly. No way was I going to work this hard only to lose by a hair's breadth!

"LET'S GO!" I screamed across the gym. Jason needed to hurry unless we wanted to go home as losers. Something about winning the team WOD makes Saturdays better, and we wanted this win. Because we *could* win. It was totally possible.

The intensity continued to escalate as we fought through the workout. In spite of our exhaustion, we pushed through every movement with more vigor than the one before. We barked orders at each other like we were on a literal battlefield, intent on winning.

Finally, we knocked out the last rep of the last exercise. It was over. The WOD was complete ...

And we had won.

We may have been victorious, but there was no victory lap around the gym—not even a winning dance. All our energy spent, we collapsed onto the dirty gym floor. There we lay, barely able to breathe. But despite our heaving chests, red faces, and sweat-soaked clothes, we were happy.

We were complete.

We were together.

"Great job, Babe," Jason said as he rolled over, stretching toward me for a fist bump.

"Yeah, that was awesome!" I responded as I touched fists with him. "Good work!"

One of our fellow CrossFitters walked by. The slogan on his T-shirt perfectly declared the sentiment of the day: "More is accomplished in the pain cave than the comfort zone."

On this day we walked straight into the pain cave, punched the "pain grizzly" in the face, fought him for thirty minutes, and came out victorious ... together.

On the car ride home, I felt almost euphoric. The workout had cleared our minds and cleansed our bodies. More importantly, working hard toward a common goal had bonded us. That morning, we had been battle buddies, complete with genuine respect for each other and sincere appreciation for the effort we had just put in together. The moment had drawn us together. We felt close.

This must be how a band of brothers in the army feels after a long, hard-fought battle, I thought to myself.

That's when it hit me. We had just been shouting at each other, pushing one another to the brink of breaking, and yet here we were feeling so connected.

"It's funny that we talk so intensely to each other in a workout like that and never think a thing of it," I said as we drove home. "We don't usually end intense conversations at home with 'that was awesome' and a fist bump."

Jason nodded in agreement. I could see the wheels turning in his mind as he thought about what I had just said. We were almost in our driveway before he broke the silence.

"Yeah, because in CrossFit, we know we're in a fight and have to work together if we're going to win," he said. "The goal is clearly defined. If we just play off each other right, strategizing our strengths and weaknesses, we have a better chance of winning. Getting offended with each other would only be a distraction." Jason paused a second before stating the obvious, "It would be stupid."

It was simple.

It wasn't rocket science.

Fighting together drew us together. As long as we recognized we were on the same team in a fight with a clearly defined goal, we could win.

WOD #2

A few minutes later, we were back home where our four kids waited. This, we always joke, is when our second WOD begins. Talk about a pain cave! Six human beings with different personalities under one roof is a workout, indeed.

This Saturday, all four kids were struggling in some way. It felt like everyone was up in arms about some issue or another. I can't even recall the exact problems, but things escalated so quickly that Jason and I ended up arguing about how to solve them. All our earlier camaraderie was long gone. In this moment, the only "fist-bump" I wanted to give him would be sure to leave a mark.

Words flew from both sides, and none of them were "awesome job" or "good work." In that moment everything was offensive—even Jason's breath, if I recall correctly. He needed a mint (or five) and all I could think was that I wished he would take his dragon breath and his opinions and find a real bike to pedal furiously—far away from me. (*Jason*: Now that is some quality trash talk. Bravo!)

Yet in that moment, a realization dawned. Jason was still talking about the kids' situation, but my mind drifted back to the conversation we'd had on the way home.

Somehow, in all our passion of the moment, we were missing the reality of the situation. We were on the same team! We wanted the same thing! The two of us had the same goal for our kids and our family. Yet, instead of moving toward that goal together, we were stuck in a pattern we hated but could not seem to break out of. This pattern of fighting against each other, instead of alongside one another, was killing us.

We were wasting time and expending energy going at each other when we should have been coordinating our efforts and winning the most important battle in our lives—the spiritual battle for the hearts and souls of our kids.

Looking back, I realize that God was giving me this moment of clarity. Somehow, I had lost sight of the real goal. When did Jason's weaknesses start to matter more to me than his strengths? How had I become so distracted with petty things that were keeping us from fighting through to victory? How had we turned into adversaries within our own marriage?

As my thinking began to change, so did my posture. I could feel my jaw loosen and my gaze soften. It became obvious to me. Our two "WODs" were playing out so differently, and the one that really mattered was the one we were losing!

My animosity faded as truth invaded my heart.

"We both want the same thing here, don't we?" I asked, trying to calm the situation. "You love our kids as much as I do. Ultimately, we want the same thing."

Jason shifted his weight and I could tell he was listening.

"We may disagree on how to best work this out," I said,

"but we disagreed on lots of things during the CrossFit WOD this morning. Ultimately, that struggle drew us together, because we were on the same team and knew what our goal was. We knew we were in a fight and had to work together."

Right there in the middle of our confrontation, something changed. Suddenly, Jason's flaws seemed to diminish, and his strengths began to look more like assets than threats. I was no longer seeing him as my domestic rival, but as my teammate. The reality was obvious; we *were* a great team ... not just at the gym but at home as well. Somehow, we had lost sight of that. Not only was it costing us our peace, but ultimately it was going to affect our kids.

We realized that day that the two of us *together* could totally win this battle for our kids and our marriage—the relationships we cherished the most. This was not a personal battle between Jason and me. It was a spiritual battle between us and the enemy of our family.

In order to win, we needed to see the battle for what it really was: Satan trying to divide and defeat us. Our whole world changed when God transformed our way of viewing our marriage. And, as Jason said earlier in the car, it felt "stupid" to move toward victory any other way.

My father-in-law often says, "How you see the battle determines how you fight it!" That day, while in the midst of trench warfare, we saw the battle for what it was—a spiritual fight we could win.

By God's grace, our marriage has never been the same. We realized we were fighting against each other in a personal battle when we should've been fighting alongside one another in a spiritual war. Thankfully, in this Kingdom struggle, God has promised us victory.

That day will always remind us of one of the most powerful truths we've ever learned in marriage: fighting together draws us together when we know what we're fighting for and who we're fighting against.

We came out of that situation feeling closer and more intimately connected than ever before. God had put us in the pain cave that day—not once but twice—and the mindset from the first showed us how to win the second. All it took was a pivot from fighting face-to-face to fighting shoulder-to-shoulder. And it turns out that winning together in life has the same enticing power as winning together in CrossFit: It keeps you coming back for more.

When you see marriage like this, everything changes.

KEY TAKEAWAY:

Fighting together draws you together when you realize that you're in a battle, you know what you're fighting for, and you know who you're fighting against.

QUESTIONS FOR CLOSER CONNECTION.
ASK YOUR SPOUSE:

1. Tell me about a time when you were aware that I was your partner in an external "battle" of some sort.

2. What about a time when I turned against you?

3. The next time we're faced with the choice to fight against each other or fight alongside each other in a stressful situation, how can I best remind you that we are in this together?

CHAPTER 2

A NEW PAIR OF GLASSES

"If you want small changes in your life, work on your attitude.
But if you want lasting and primary changes,
work on your paradigm."
– Stephen Covey

Jason:

How you *see* determines how you *act*. When perception changes, behavior changes. We discovered this profound truth through the sport of CrossFit, but it's also true in marriage. The single best thing we've ever done for our relationship was to change the way we *viewed* it.

Our goal is not to simply give you another how-to book that focuses on behavior change. While books like that are helpful—and we've read many of them—our focus is *paradigm* change. We want to give you a new lens through which you can view your spouse and the relationship you have together.

We've seen firsthand the power of this shift in perspective in our own marriage, and we've seen it happen to others in the process of our marriage ministry. As we counsel couples sitting on our living room couch, we've discovered that if we can get them to *see* differently, their behavior toward each other will change naturally.

When I was younger, my dad got a birthday gift from a

woman in the congregation he pastored. When he opened it, he thought it was a joke because it was an 8x10 frame containing a picture of nothing but dots—thousands of them.

She explained that it was a random-dot stereogram. An image was buried beneath all the dots; if you looked long enough, the picture would emerge.

"Oh, just wait until you see the picture," she said with a smile. "It will take some time, but when you see it, you'll like it."

Dad set the picture on his big wooden desk in front of the double window in our den. That's where he prepared his Sunday messages. Occasionally I would see him stare at the picture for a few minutes, but never for too long. He'd just shake his head and go back to typing up his sermon.

For the next several weeks, right after every service, the woman would approach my dad and ask, "Did you see it yet, Pastor Flip?"

"Not yet," Dad would reply. "But I'm trying."

"Don't try so hard," she said one afternoon. "If you just relax your eyes, you'll see it."

That week, Dad determined to see the image behind the dots. He couldn't face one more Sunday telling her he didn't see it. So, he sat at his desk, took the picture in his hands and stared at it for several minutes. Remembering what she had said, he relaxed his eyes until the dots blurred together on the page.

At that moment, something amazing happened: Out of the mass of dots, three crosses emerged in 3D. It caught him so much by surprise that he set the picture down and looked away, just to make sure he wasn't hallucinating. When he looked again, the crosses were still there.

When Sunday rolled around, Dad was finally able to tell the generous church member what he had seen.

"I knew you would," she said. "But the best part is that, once you see the picture, you can never *un-see* it. You'll never see just dots again."

From that point on, when Dad would look at that picture,

the cross of Christ would jump out of those dots every time. When he showed it to my brother and me, we never saw anything. Neither of us had the patience to sit and stare at it long enough. Yet my Dad now had eyes to see through all the dots. Although nothing in the picture had changed, everything was different.

That little story exemplifies what we hope for you and your marriage. We want you to see the picture behind all the dots—a picture God has painted of what your marriage *could* be and what it *should* be. Lasting change in marriage is only possible when you change the lens through which you view your relationship. The beauty of changing the way you see is that your behavior will change as a natural outgrowth of this shift in perspective.

This is what took place for Tori and me. We'd read lots of "how-to" books on marriage and put their advice into practice. Much of it was helpful, yet our behavior modifications were short-lived. We'd always drift back into old, negative behavior patterns. This outside-in approach aimed at changing behavior, while helpful to some degree, did not give us the lasting change we needed.

It wasn't until we changed the way we *saw* our relationship that we experienced the depth of intimacy we now enjoy. We no longer had to "try" anymore because our behavior changed from the inside out. Like the random-dot stereogram, once the image was made clear, it couldn't be unseen. When we saw differently, we felt differently, and our actions followed naturally.

Jesus mentioned this powerful truth when He said, "The Son can do nothing by Himself; He can only do what He *sees* His Father doing ..." (John 5:19, emphasis added). If the actions of the Savior were fueled by what He saw, how much more should this hold true for us?

The way you see influences the way you feel.

And the way you feel influences the way you act.

I heard a true story about a businessman on the subway in New York City who was peacefully riding to church one Sunday morning. He and other passengers sat quietly, reading the paper or waiting for their stop. Then a dad with three small kids entered the subway car. The moment they stepped in, the kids started yelling, throwing things, and running around the car—upsetting the once-peaceful atmosphere.

The dad sat there with his eyes closed, oblivious to the whole thing.

Clearly agitated, the businessman looked over at the dad and said, "Sir, your children are disturbing people. I wonder if you couldn't control them a little more?"

The dad looked up as if he were surprised at his kids' behavior. "Oh, you're right," he said softly. "I guess I should do something about it. We just came from the hospital where their mother died about an hour ago. I don't know what to do, and I guess they don't know how to handle it either."

At that moment, everything changed. This flustered businessman who had seen these kids as obnoxious and the dad as oblivious now viewed them through a lens of compassion rather than frustration. As a result, he was no longer angry, but broken over their situation. He didn't need a how-to list or a step-by-step process on how to help a hurting person. The compassion in his heart propelled him to act. He instinctively knew what to do because he saw the situation differently.

"Oh, Sir," the businessman responded. "I'm so sorry! What can I do to help?"

Although nothing in the situation had changed, everything was different once he knew the truth behind the circumstances.[1]

Satan hates the truth. He is the author of lies. He would have loved for that man to continue to view the situation through the lens of anger and self-righteousness rather than the lens of love. All he had to do was keep him in the dark about the truth. That would have kept him in a posture of fighting face-to-face against an oblivious dad rather than shoulder-to-shoulder alongside a broken husband.

We want you to see your relationship differently, as the

businessman did on that subway car and as my dad did with that 3D picture. We want you to see what God says about marriage and what He feels about your partner. If you discover the truth about marriage—why God made it and what purpose it serves— you'll treat your own relationship differently.

If you discover the truth about your spouse—how God is not just your Father but also your Father-in-Law—your actions toward His son or daughter will line up with His intentions for them. Although the circumstances in your relationship may be the same, everything will be different.

The relationship Tori and I share is living proof that change is possible and probable when this truth comes into focus. Through a series of events, God radically transformed the way we saw each other and the way we viewed our marriage. When we realized we didn't have to stop fighting—and that our marriage was actually *made* for a fight—our lives were transformed. This new lens allowed us to see each other not as enemies at war but as buddies in battle. Entering it together drew us together.

You might think this kind of paradigm shift is impossible. Perhaps you and your spouse have developed deep-rutted routines over time that have you gritting your teeth and facing off against your partner about daily issues, large and small. So, before we dive in, we want to offer you some encouragement from Jesus about the truly transformational power of having eyes to see.

Before He went to the cross, Jesus told His disciples, "A little while, and you will not *see* Me, and again a little while, and you will *see* Me. Truly, truly, I say to you, that you will weep and lament, but the world will rejoice; you will grieve, but your grief will be turned into joy" (John 16:19-20, emphasis added).

Jesus knew the time of His death was near and the disciples would no longer see Him, which would result in their grief. But He promised that their grief would be turned to joy because they would see Him once again after He rose from the grave. Although the disciples didn't understand it at the moment, they eventually realized what He'd been talking about when it happened.

Their story shows us an incredible principle we can use to strengthen our own relationships: grief is transformed into joy when you *see* Jesus in the struggle. This is the real beauty in battle—seeing Jesus in the midst of the fight.

Seeing Him changes everything.

Truth is, if you desire to see Jesus in the midst of your fight, He will emerge from the dots. He is just as excited to rekindle that romantic flame in your relationship as He is to raise the dead and heal the sick. He is all about mending broken things and bringing the Kingdom of God into the world.

Hold onto Him and don't lose hope. Cling to Him in faith and let Him breathe new life into your relationship. Depend on Him to mend the brokenness of your marriage and transform your home into a little bit of the Kingdom here on earth. He will do it for you just as He did it for us … and we can't wait to share with you how He did it!

KEY TAKEAWAY:

Lasting change in marriage is only possible when you change the lens through which you view your relationship. When your perspective changes, behavior naturally follows.

QUESTIONS FOR CLOSER CONNECTION. ASK YOUR SPOUSE:

1. Do you see me the same way you did when we were dating? If not, what has changed?
2. Do my actions make you feel like I see you in a negative light? What actions do you want me to stop? What would you like me to do more of?
3. Have we truly made Jesus the center of our relationship? Where are you in your relationship with Him?

CHAPTER 3

A VISION OF US

"The only thing worse than being blind is
having sight but no vision."
– Helen Keller

Jason:

We have this massive magnolia tree outside our house that drops leaves like I used to drop buckets in high school basketball—frequently and plentifully. The only problem is that they are massive, and they don't disintegrate like normal leaves. If we don't rake them up, they'll lie around … forever.

It's the worst in the spring when a storm hits just about every week. If the wind picks up even just a little, it throws those nasty banana boats all over our yard, leaving me and my incredibly sensitive OCD in an absolute state of frenzy.

Yesterday was one such day. Tori and I were sitting on our back patio watching our two youngest (and just about every other kid from the neighborhood) swim in the pool. Tori was on a roll talking about something while I sat there fighting off thoughts like, *If one of those kids pees in my pool, I will* _____ (you fill in the blank).

The weather was so nice I asked Tori if she'd like to have dinner outside later that night. She loved the idea and started making preparations. Family dinners are just about the only time we and our kids can all be together in one spot, so we try to guard that time as best we can. The older our kids get, the more difficult it is for us to pull it off. As of the writing of this book, we have a nineteen-year-old boy, a seventeen-year-old girl, a fifteen-year-old boy, and an eleven-year-old girl all under one roof. (God help us.)

But yesterday, there was a problem. A storm had hit two days earlier and there were magnolia leaves all over the patio. I had been in agony over these little monsters for the last forty-eight hours, knowing I needed to clean them up, but I had nothing pushing me to do it ... until then. There was no way I could actually relax and enjoy dinner with these roof shingles everywhere.

As Tori was working her dinner magic, I saw a clear picture in my mind of our family sitting around the table under our little pergola on a clean patio. It wasn't like some big vision or anything, but just a small thought of how nice dinner would be outside with all the kids ... in an orderly environment.

The minute I saw that picture in my mind, I jumped off my chair, yelled at a few of the boys bobbing around in the pool to come help, and off we went picking up the monster leaves. Fifteen minutes later, everything was done. What I had procrastinated on for two days was complete in less than a half hour.

Seeing that picture in my mind of a clean patio reminded me of the times we put jigsaw puzzles together with our kids when they were young. The picture on the box guided us as we tried to make sense of all the tiny pieces strewn all over the table—it gave us a vision of what could be and kept us moving toward what should be.

Last night, we had dinner on our patio. It was fun. The place was clean. And I was able to relax and enjoy it all, even though our daughter Lundi confessed at the table that she had peed in the pool. "But just a little."

As we discussed in the last chapter, changing your paradigm is about opening your eyes to the truth of your present reality. When God gives you new eyes to see your spouse and your marriage everything changes. Establishing vision, however, takes it one step further. Having a vision for your relationship is about seeing a potential future that has yet to be realized. If you want a thriving marriage to become a reality, then you have to first see it in your mind.

The wisest man who ever lived once said this about vision, "Where there is no vision, the people perish" (Proverbs 29:18). That sage wisdom came from the mouth of the greatest activator of all time, King Solomon. He was the guy who turned his dad's vision of the Temple into a reality.

Without a vision for your marriage it will die. Vision is the fuel for passion, which gives you the energy to do the thing you see in your mind. You'll never engage in the battle for your relationship if you don't first have a vision for it.

Tori:

When we were young, we had a vision for what our marriage would be like. We'd picture it in our minds and daydream about it. But then we got married and the dream began to fade as more "important things" like work and bills and ballgames and "all the things" set in.

But we didn't do "all the things" we thought we'd do—the fun stuff we always said we'd do. We didn't dance in the kitchen anymore or stay up late and talk or eat Chinese food as we watched Hugh Grant romantic comedies.

We didn't do the things we wanted to do because we no longer had the passion that gave us the energy to execute those things.

Why? Because somewhere along the way, we lost sight

of our original dream. We lost the vision we once had for our relationship.

For me, the *vision* of us had been replaced with the *reality* of us. And the reality of where we were—with four young kids and no time to do anything but … well … scream—left us often feeling hopeless.

Looking back, it was during those times when a *vision* for our marriage could have energized us to make it through the *reality* of our marriage. Losing sight of our dream sucked the life right out of us. The picture was there, of course. We just weren't looking at it.

When we dated, we were massively energized for "us" because we visualized the beauty of what could be ours. But over time, we gradually drifted into a routine and forgot how to dream. It took a physical dream to wake us up to the dream we had forgotten. And when we got it back, it filled us with passion and energy to move toward the marriage we had once hoped for.

Jason:

Studies show that the part of your brain that activates when you *visualize* an action is the same that activates when you actually *do* the action.[2] Your brain has a difficult time distinguishing between what you see with your physical eyes and what you see in your mind. MRI scans show the brain activity for someone watching a sunset is the same as someone visualizing it in their mind.[3]

This is the power of the imagination that you tap into when you visualize something. Your brain doesn't know if it's real or imaginary, so you begin to think and act as if it's true. It's what mega movie star Jim Carrey did before he became famous: He wrote a million-dollar check to himself and kept it in his wallet long before he ever earned that much from a movie.[4]

I know this may sound technical, and you're probably wondering what in the world this has to do with marriage …

but stick with me. The breakthroughs in science that show the power of visualization and its effect on the brain have helped me and Tori tremendously in our marriage. Science is finally catching up with the Bible!

The reason visualization is so powerful is because it taps into your subconscious to help you realize the thing you see in your mind. You don't have to know how to get there because your subconscious will do a lot of the work. It does so by tapping into the reticular activating system (RAS) of your brain. I call it the "brain filter."

Your subconscious mind processes about fifty thousand thoughts a day, most of which never make it to your conscious mind. The RAS is the filter that separates your conscious thoughts from the subconscious ones and determines which get through and which don't.

The RAS takes what you focus on and creates a filter for it, then sifts through the data and only presents the pieces that are important to you. All of this happens without you even noticing.[5]

This is what takes place when you buy a certain kind of car and then start seeing that model everywhere, even though you never noticed it before. Once you bought it, your RAS notified your brain that this particular car was significant and now triggers when you see it elsewhere.

If you focus hard on your goals, visualizing what you want to accomplish, your RAS will reveal the opportunities to help you make it a reality. If having an incredible marriage laced with romance is significant to you, then opportunities to make it a reality will present themselves and you'll have the desire and energy to make it happen.

If you don't have a vision for your marriage like this, then desire and energy will be replaced with apathy and lethargy, the twin killers of relationship. If this describes your marriage, ask God to give you a jolt in the right direction. He did it for me with a crazy dream (that story is coming!).

And he can do it for you too. Maybe not with a dream,

but in the way and with the means He knows will work for you. He's got the time, and He's got the desire to bring you and your spouse closer together than ever—because this is what you need in order to be effective partners fighting side by side.

Your subconscious mind is at work twenty-four hours a day, seven days a week, doing exactly what you tell it to do. You feed it instructions by visualizing what you want as if it has already happened.[6] Most married couples tapped into this incredible power—without even knowing it—before they got married. It's what moved them to get married in the first place. But then life hits and our dream of what could be and should be drifts into our subconscious and is forgotten.

But you can get it back. You can recover that long-lost dream and regain the vision you once had for your relationship. Tori and I have found three keys that keep our vision of *us* front-and-center and allow our brain filters to make it a reality:

- <u>Want It:</u> Do we really want the best marriage possible?
- <u>Believe It:</u> Do we really believe we can have an incredible marriage?
- <u>Focus on It:</u> Are we willing to focus on the things that will make it a reality?

We choose to *want* the marriage we once dreamed about. We choose to *believe* that, with God's help, we can achieve it. And we choose to *focus* on our vision of us above all else.

King Solomon was right. Without vision, people die. Without vision for your marriage, without reigniting that dream you once had for your relationship, passion fades and the energy you once had will evaporate, leaving you with a shell of the marriage you once dreamed about.

But *it doesn't have to be this way*. The passion and energy you need can be reignited when you re-establish the importance of your vision of marriage. Having vision for your marriage sees victory before it ever comes. You won't need a "how to" guide to show you what to do. You'll instinctively know how to make it a reality because that's the way God wired you.

Tori:

There's a scene in the movie *The Notebook* (one of my favorite movies, I admit) where Noah discovers that his long-lost sweetheart, Allie, is engaged to another man. Just before the wedding, Allie goes to visit Noah to finally put their relationship to rest. Both of them are still madly in love with each other, but neither one of them realizes it (or is willing to accept it).

In the middle of a heated exchange, Noah says, "Will you do something for me, please? Picture your life for me, thirty years from now. What's it look like? If it's with that guy, go! I lost you once. I think I could do it again, if I thought it's what you really wanted ... stop thinking about what everybody else wants ... what do you want?"

This is my favorite scene in the movie because the two are fighting like they always do, but Noah makes it clear he's fighting *for* Allie. And he knows that Allie needs to see the future as he sees it if they're going to make it work.

We move toward that in which we focus. With three teen-age drivers in our home at the moment, nothing feels more true. Without a clear picture of what you want for your marriage, the chances of you achieving it is slim to none.

Jason and I use a little phrase whenever we find ourselves feeling disconnected from each other after a disagreement. One of us will say, "I wanna be in *us*." That's code for, "Let's be what we should be." We can't get back into *us* if we don't have a clear picture of what that looks like.

This is how you can redirect a knock-down-drag-out fight between yourselves and unite as one to fight against the common enemy who wants nothing more than for you to continue to destroy each other. You can even do it right now as you read this book.

If an awesome marriage is what you want, and both of you believe it can happen and you're willing to focus on your vision of *us*, then you will move toward it.

"A Vision of *Us*."

This little phrase is a reminder that vision in marriage is a lot like the lid of a jigsaw puzzle—it gives you a clear picture of what could be and what should be for your relationship. It's there for you to see. All you have to do is start looking at it again.

KEY TAKEAWAY:

Without a vision for your marriage it will die. Vision is the fuel for passion, which gives you the energy to do the thing you see in your mind. Remember back to your original vision for your relationship, then *want* it, *believe* it can happen, and *focus on* it to make it a reality.

QUESTIONS FOR CLOSER CONNECTION. DISCUSS TOGETHER:

1. What was our original vision for our marriage?
2. Have we lost site of it?
3. Do we want it back?
4. How are we going to get it back and keep it alive?

CHAPTER 4

LEAVE THE SUITCASE

*"Difficulties are meant to rouse, not discourage.
The human spirit is to grow strong by conflict."*
– William Ellery Channing

Tori:

Unfortunately, no amount of vision will keep the gusty winds of conflict from sweeping through your relationship. In the early days of our marriage, Jason and I had not yet learned that conflict is actually a good thing, and that God uses marriage to provide the context for the clash to take place. Conflicts give us the opportunity to die to ourselves as we choose to love our spouse when he or she is … well … *not so loveable.*

It didn't take long before those gusty winds came howling our way.

We had been married all of ninety-six hours when Jason threw our green suitcase across the room. Up to that point, our young marriage had been everything we had dreamed about. Sleeping in while snuggling up, endless conversation in the Jacuzzi tub, late-night movies in bed—all the fun stuff we told each other we couldn't wait to do on our honeymoon. We were getting along just fine.

The morning after our wedding, a few days before the suitcase ordeal, we woke up to a blizzard. It was the worst snowstorm to hit the Northeast in over a decade. Connecticut was pounded with four feet of snow in one day.

We didn't take it as a sign from God that our own relational storm was on its way. We just thought it was God's way of keeping us around a little longer before we headed out for our honeymoon.

Jason:

When the storm subsided, we flew down to Florida's South Beach for a few nights, then headed to the Bahamas on a cruise. I could hear the theme song from *The Love Boat* ringing in my ears as we boarded the ship. I was on cloud nine, anticipating what I assumed would be a perfect honeymoon.

I made the rookie mistake of booking the cheapest cabin I could find. When we showed up and opened the door, we found a room that looked like it was made for one of Santa's elves. It was the size of a decent master closet. The bathroom looked and smelled like it came out of a commercial airplane. There were two smaller-than-normal twin beds on either side of the room.

"Oh, heck no!" I said. "I'm going to fix this right now!" I immediately pushed the beds together.

The boat wouldn't leave for a few hours, so we ran around like two little kids at Disney World. We checked out the restaurants and the pools and the workout room and the hot tubs and the all-you-can-stand buffet that hadn't yet opened. We even found the layout spot on the upper deck (but exited as quickly as we'd entered when we discovered it was topless). I vaguely remember Tori threatening to take my life through asphyxiation if I went up there. (I had to Google that word.)

Finally, we settled down in a few deck chairs with our feet

propped up on the boat railing. We breathed in the crisp ocean air as the boat weighed anchor and slowly drifted out to sea.

Life couldn't get any better. That is, until Tori leaned over a few minutes later in the "I think I'm going to barf" position.

"Uh-oh," she said. "I don't feel good."

"Really?" I asked. "Did you eat something?"

"I get motion sickness," she said, placing her hands on her stomach. "This boat rocking is killing me."

Another rookie mistake—I never checked with Tori about the whole "motion sick" thing before I booked a cruise for our honeymoon.

We immediately went back to the cabin, where Tori locked herself in the tiny bathroom. Every few minutes I'd hear her heave into the toilet, followed by a violent flush that sounded like the vacuum of a jet engine.

Poor girl, I thought as I lay on that munchkin bed listening to her moaning. *I wonder if she'll be ready for dinner in an hour?*

I was fresh out of pro baseball, so my metabolism was still cranking away. Food was just about all I thought about (as a newly married man, it wasn't *all* I thought about!). The longer Tori stayed in the bathroom, the hungrier I got. And the more I focused on all the amazing food I was missing out on, the more I thought about me and the less I thought about her.

"Hey, Honey," I said, masking my hangriness with a tone of concern. "You doing okay in there?"

"Be out—" cough, cough, heave, flush, "—in a minute," she said.

Finally, after about an hour in the john, she emerged.

"I think I'm going to lie down," she said. "But I know you're hungry, so you go get something without me."

But I didn't want to eat alone on my honeymoon. I wanted to eat with her.

"Can't you just take a few more of those seasick pills you bought earlier?" I asked, not wanting to give up my plan for an incredibly romantic evening.

"No—they make me too groggy." She dismissed my idea without a second thought. "I'm just going to lie here a bit."

Then she drifted off to sleep.

Well, if you are going to sleep anyway, why not try the stinkin' pills? I thought to myself.

Everything I envisioned for our honeymoon seemed to be slowly fading away. But my stomach overruled my emotions, so I walked to the dining area alone, scarfed down as much food as humanly possible, then went back to the room to be with Tori.

End of Day One.

On Day Two, she felt much better as we pulled into port and hung out in Nassau. But when we re-boarded the ship and it began to rock, seasickness hit her all over again. I found myself starting to get a little frustrated. I wasn't mad at her; I was frustrated at the situation. My expectations for the most romantic honeymoon ever was quickly being replaced by a flushing toilet and sleeping wife. It was the unmet expectation of what my time with her was *supposed* to look like that upset me.

Of course, I didn't know that then. I've since discovered that unmet expectations are one of the leading causes of conflict in marriage.

At some point on Day Three, Tori started to feel better. We finally got to do all the fun stuff I'd hoped we'd do—we ate until we could hardly breathe, danced in an effort to work it off, and then relaxed by the pool to sleep it off. But when it came time for the formal dinner that night, Tori started to feel sick again. She told me she'd rather not go because she didn't think she could make it through without sprinting to the bathroom.

At that moment, I should've been a good husband and responded with empathy, putting myself in her shoes. But I wasn't a good husband at this point—I was a *new* husband. And as a newbie, I found myself getting frustrated over the whole situation. I knew it wasn't her fault, but I couldn't help feeling angry. Nothing was working out the way I wanted, the way I had expected.

But Tori was a trooper. She knew how much I wanted to go, so she found a way to power through it and satisfy her selfish husband. She put on a nice dress while I donned a suit, and we ate steak and lobster like a king and queen. Fortunately, she made it without a sprint to the bathroom.

I've since learned that an unhealthy relationship is typically characterized by tyranny from the most selfish partner. That partner has to get what they want in order for the marriage to be at peace. It makes for a terrible relatonship, let me tell ya. And on our honeymoon, I was that partner!

HEARTBURN

But a problem began to emerge—a heart problem. Over the course of those several days, with Tori getting sick and us missing out on some of the things I had planned, I found myself growing more and more insensitive toward her. The day before the cruise was over, we found ourselves getting into a few small arguments, most of which I started. I don't even remember what they were about, but this was new territory for us. Up to that point in our relationship, we'd hardly argued. And even though I didn't like the way I was acting, I felt powerless to stop myself.

On the last day, as I began to pack our mammoth suitcase with mostly Tori's clothes, I found myself thinking, Why in the heck did she pack enough clothes to last a year on this boat? We aren't moving to flipping Gilligan's Island. This is stupid.

It hadn't occurred to me that we each could have easily brought our own suitcase. But newlyweds don't always make the wisest decisions.

Of course, I couldn't keep any of these negative thoughts to myself, and I had no intention of focusing on the good in her when all the bad was consuming me.

"Are you serious with all these clothes?" I asked. "This is crazy."

"Why does it matter?" she said.

"You don't have to lug all this junk around everywhere," I snapped.

"Fine. Give it to me then!" she snapped back. "I'll take it."

And with that, I flung the suitcase full of her clothes across the room.

Right then and there, I erased all doubt that Tori had married a moron. I'm still surprised she didn't slap me to my senses.

GO THROUGH IT

Tori:

What I remember most about our honeymoon experience is that I had gone from the high of being a beautiful bride on a trajectory to make all Jason's dreams come true to the low of a powerless wife stuck in bed making her new husband miserable. It was a lot to work out, to say the least.

Little did I know that our first major conflict as a married couple would reveal two underlying issues both of us needed to address: Jason's need to control and my propensity to stonewall or withdraw when feeling controlled.

My nephew, Tripp, had a favorite book I use to read him on our family beach vacations. It's titled *We're Going on a Bear Hunt* and the catchy phrase repeated throughout the adventure is, "We can't go over it. We can't go under it. Oh, no! We've got to go through it!"

That's marriage. If you want to turn conflict and chaos into passion and purpose, you have no choice but to go *through* the struggle to get to the other side. And when you do, you'll be stronger than you were before.

Early in our marriage, if I could make Jason happy, I was happy. But the moment I sensed I was unable to, a sense of hopelessness would invade my spirit. Meanwhile, my emotional awareness of what was transpiring was at a zero. I had no idea why I was feeling so overwhelmed. So, while I would eventually "get over it," I never actually arrived on the other side where I could be healthy and whole. It was a vicious emotional cycle.

I've heard it said that insanity is doing the same thing over and over but expecting a different result. I guess you could say I was insane during the first few years of marriage. Tripp's little book was right: *We can't go over it. We can't go under it … we have to go through it.*

But truly going through it means gaining strength from the struggle to get to the other side. It's more than just a willingness to go through it; you also have to learn from it. Otherwise, you'll end up repeating the same struggles over and over again without anything to show for it on the other side.

That first conflict in our marriage revealed a kink in my heart that God, in His kindness, wanted to work out. The moments when I felt powerless to be who I wanted to be, I would react in frustration. Sometimes I would withdraw. Other times, I would lash out.

But the conflicts that felt like they were tearing us apart from the inside had patterns. And thankfully, those patterns made us aware of the root issues for which Jason and I needed to take responsibility. God was showing me that I was putting too much pressure on myself to meet all of Jason's needs. I was left hopeless every time. I can't replace God, no matter how hard I may try.

At the same time, God was showing Jason that he was putting that pressure on me by not properly managing his expectations. And, as Jason will tell you later, he discovered that his unmet expectations would make him angry, which pointed to an even deeper issue of control.

This is the power of conflict—it reveals the intentions of the enemy and opens our eyes to the truth of the spiritual battle raging. Thankfully, God can use even our mistakes and weaknesses for His purposes, as Joseph recognized toward the end of the biblical narrative in which his being sold as a slave resulted in the salvation of a nation: "You intended to harm me, *but God* intended it for good ... " (Genesis 50:20).

Our first fight in marriage revealed things in our hearts from which God wanted to set us free. He had a purpose behind it—to make us personally and relationally stronger.

Jason:

We didn't know it then, but it was good for us to finally experience conflict. I should've remembered all the times my professors in graduate school talked about the importance of conflict and how it helps shape you into the person God desires you to be. The Bible calls it "iron sharpening iron" (Proverbs 27:17). But when the sparks are flying, it's not an enjoyable process.

What Tori and I have learned since that first fight is that marriage ultimately isn't about you and your spouse—it's about you and Jesus. God uses conflict to make us more like Jesus. It gives us the opportunity to respond as He responds, love like He loves, and forgive like He forgives.

Have you ever noticed how many verses in the Bible talk about "others"? You probably know it's filled with verses about all the good things we should do for other people, but have you ever considered that the primary "other" in your life is your spouse? We tend to apply these verses to poor people or strangers or even enemies. But for every verse you read about *others,* you should put your spouse's picture right next to it.

Jesus taught that whatever we do to the "least of these," we've done to Him (Matthew 25:40). Whenever your spouse says or does something stupid or hurtful (like I did in the first days of our marriage), they become "the least of these" in that moment. This is your opportunity to respond as Jesus would respond, to love like He loves, and to forgive as He forgives.

As we said earlier, marriage provides the context for conflict, which in turn enables us to learn how to live and love sacrificially.

Jesus gave some of the best marriage advice of all whe
"Whoever wants to be my disciple must deny them.
take up their cross and follow me" (Matthew 16:24). *
a place of death. We shouldn't pick it up unless we're w....ng to
die. Conflict gives us the opportunity to die to ourselves as we
continue to love our spouse when he or she has become "the least
of these."

PLEASING THE IN-LAWS

Here's something you need to remember: God is not just
your Father. He's your Father-*in-Law*.[7] As such, the best thing
you can do for Him is to love His son or daughter.

As parents, we know what this kind of fatherly or motherly
love feels like. You know the best way someone can bless you is
by blessing your kids. But kids are squirrelly, so we know they're
going to say and do some pretty dumb things. In those moments,
if someone shows your kids grace and mercy, it draws your heart
toward that person.

The same is true in marriage. In the moments when conflict
arises, how you treat God's son or daughter is how you treat God.
This is why conflict is so important.

Gary Thomas, in his bestselling book *Sacred Marriage*,
writes, "Marriage isn't to make you happy. It's to make you
holy. Conflict provides the path for spiritual growth."[8] A holy
life cannot be experienced apart from the struggle that makes us
holy. Marriage is the context for that struggle. It refines us more
into His image. Like sandpaper, conflict is unpleasant, but it will
smooth out the rough edges … in time.

That last day on the boat revealed there was something
deep inside me that had not manifested itself until this conflict
with Tori. While my unmet expectations had fueled my frustration earlier on the trip, my desire for control fueled it when we
were about to leave. Until then, the only suitcase I'd ever had to
pack was my own, so I controlled what went inside it. But now,

packing a suitcase full of clothes that I thought didn't need to be in it made me feel out of control, so I snapped.

I know it sounds petty, but when you think about it, most arguments *are* petty, aren't they? Thankfully, God used this conflict with Tori to point to something buried deep inside—something I didn't even know was there. He needed to stir the waters of my heart first.

The water in a small pond may look clean until you take a stick and stir up what's on the bottom, making it a muddy mess. God used Tori as the stick to stir up what was at the bottom of my heart. And it was a muddy mess.

The way a couple handles conflict sets the course for their entire relationship. Since that time, and in countless meetings with other couples, we have talked a lot about the value of conflict and how to leverage it so you grow closer to each other rather than further apart.

When conflict arises, two things always manifest themselves:

1. The issue to be dealt with
2. Each person's ability to deal with the issue

If number two is good, then number one will usually take care of itself.[9]

Ability is spelled R-E-S-P-O-N-S-I-B-I-L-I-T-Y. Taking responsibility for your part in the conflict is always the first thing that needs to happen. Interestingly, modern psychiatry labels those who refuse to observe their own problems, take responsibility, and accept feedback from others as having "character disorders."[10]

The real issue for me and Tori was not that she got sick or that she had packed too much. The real issue was my unmet expectations and my desire for control. For her, it was trying to be all things to me and operating out of hopelessness when she couldn't. These heart problems created gaps between us. And ultimately, reconnection could only be found on the other side of taking responsibility for our part.

SEE IT

One of the best ways we've learned to harness conflict for our advantage is to see it differently. We no longer see conflict as something we need to *resolve*, but something we should *manage*. If we try to resolve it, we try to fix it, which often leads us to seek to control the situation or win our spouse to our way of thinking. While you may win the argument, you won't win the person. Relational disconnection is always the result.

Much of the conflict we experience is not over easily resolvable issues. For instance, Tori still packs way too much—in my humble opinion! But I'm learning that when I try to understand her way of thinking instead of trying to win her to mine, we draw closer through the conflict.

I mean, I still don't *really* understand why she thinks all that stuff is necessary, but I do understand her desire to be prepared. Hey, if our plane is going down and it looks like we might be stranded on an island for a year, I want Tori's fifty-pound bag with us.

Instead of fearing conflict, many couples can find growth and healing if they understand that it will actually draw them closer together if they learn to properly harness its power. Simply recognizing this fact is one of the first steps to take when turning conflict into something that strengthens you rather than separates you.

By the way, we still have the suitcase I flung across that tiny cruise ship cabin. It sits in our shed as a reminder of the value of conflict and how God used it—and uses it still—to strengthen our marriage.

KEY TAKEAWAY:

Your marriage ultimately isn't about you and your spouse—it's about you and Jesus. God uses conflict to make us more like Jesus. It gives us the opportunity to respond as He responds, love like He loves, and forgive like He forgives.

QUESTIONS FOR CLOSER CONNECTION. ASK YOUR SPOUSE:

1. How do you feel some of the conflicts we've endured have "sharpened" you?
2. What core issue has conflict shed light on in you?
3. How can I best support you as you work through it personally?

CHAPTER 5

WEDDING CRASHER

"The great dragon was hurled down—that ancient serpent called
the devil, or Satan, who leads the whole world astray.
He was hurled to the earth, and his angels with him."
– Revelation 12:9

Jason:

Before we move further, I want to pause and look at the
Biblical foundation for why conflict exists and why we chose to
write about marriage within the context of a fight. What I will
share with you in this brief chapter is the reason we chose the title
Beauty in Battle. When you see what's taking place in the spiritual realm and how this whole battle began in the first place, it
will open your eyes to the importance of your marriage and why
fighting together is so important … and so powerful.

Have you ever noticed how Scripture opens and closes with
a wedding? It starts with a marriage in Genesis where Adam is
the groom and Eve is the bride, and it ends in Revelation where
Jesus is the groom and the Church is His bride. Marriage is so
important to God that it bookends human history.

But one thing you may not have noticed was that the first

marriage had an uninvited guest, a wedding crasher who wanted nothing more than to be a marriage smasher. This wedding crasher's name is Satan and knowing how he got there is where the story of marriage begins.

If we were to ask you, "What was the first sin?" what would you say?

When Eve ate the fruit, right? (That's what we said.)

But the first sin actually took place in Heaven when Satan wanted God's throne and tried to take it from Him. He didn't like the fact that God was the only One in charge, and felt he was better equipped for the job. He desperately wanted God's authority—and he was prideful enough to fight for it (Revelation 12:7-9).

How did God deal with this? An epic battle in heaven took place where Satan and his band of hooligan angels got their butts smacked.

But here's where the story turns. You would think God would destroy Satan once and for all, but that's not what He did. He chose, rather, to cast him out of Heaven to a place called... Earth.

At some point after this heavenly fight, God created Adam. Where did God put him? In the very place He had put Satan—Earth!

WHOA. God just put Adam in the same spot as the banished angel who wanted to take His throne. Even better, God gave Adam authority as ruler—the very thing Satan wanted when he was in Heaven.

It's as if God set the stage for an epic showdown or something—like a cage fight!

But God, knowing Satan would go after Adam's authority just as he went after His, would not leave Adam out there alone, unequipped for his call and unarmed for the fight.

"So the LORD God caused a deep sleep to fall upon the man, and he slept; then He *took one of his ribs* and closed up the flesh at that place. The LORD God fashioned into a woman the rib which He had taken from the man, and brought her to the man" (Genesis 2:21-22 NASB, emphasis added).

With this divine surgery, God did more than just create another human. He created *relationship* among humans, reflecting the relationship within the Godhead between Father, Son, and Holy Spirit. Eve alone was not the missing piece for Adam—a *relationship* with her was what he needed to be complete.

God designed Adam so that He would not be all that Adam needed. Adam needed a relationship with another person. Without relationship among equals, mankind could not fully reflect the image of God or fulfill His command to rule the earth.

Can you see why marriage is under attack today? Satan is nauseated by the image of God and will do everything in his power to destroy the human reflection of His image.

We were made for relationship.

Satan had yet to attack, although he had a front-row seat to Adam's divine surgery. He was also there when God presented Eve to Adam, watching for a way to get the authority he so desperately wanted.

On their wedding night, Satan saw his inroad. He noticed how Adam looked at Eve in a way he had never looked at any of the animals. In that moment, Satan moved from wedding crasher to marriage smasher.

Therein lies the paradox of marriage—the very relationship God established to *defeat* the devil is also vulnerable to his attacks.

Satan knew that unity in marriage would withstand his wiles, so he had to get these newlyweds to operate independently of each other. Together, they were an unstoppable force, created to reflect the perfection of God's image and operate in the full authority of the dominion He had gifted to them. Divided, they would be impotent and confused, literally missing half of what they had been created to be. Together, they could rule. Separated, they would be easily conquered.

Unfortunately for us, Satan's plan worked masterfully,

and we've been dealing with the fallout ever since. He disguised himself as a serpent, got into a conversation with Eve, questioned God's boundaries and goodness, and convinced her that God was holding out on them. It didn't take long, and she fell. The moment she ate the fruit, she turned and gave some to her husband, who was standing beside her (Genesis 3:6). Adam's passivity caused him lose his authority (and this has been a struggle for men ever since).

The first man and woman bought the lie of the devil, disobeyed God's clear command, and Satan ended up with what he wanted all along—authority. From that point forward, Satan became the prince of the earth (2 Corinthians 4:4, Ephesians 2:2, John 12:31).

That is, until the Second Adam—Jesus—came to fix up what the first Adam messed up (1 Corinthians 15:45). But that's jumping way ahead in the story.

Let's bring this spiritual reality to the present day … because Satan's attacks are still the same. In order to separate you from your spouse *relationally*, he first tempts you to sin against God *personally*. He does this because he knows he's just as powerless against a husband and wife united in God's name as he is against God Himself.

Why? Because when God made Adam and Eve, He didn't just form a marriage—He created a church. "And the gates of hell shall not prevail against *[the church]*" (Matthew 16:18 ESV, emphasis added).

Marriage is the most organic form of church, as it forms a union with Christ at the center: "For where two or three gather in My name, there I am with them" (Matthew 18:20).

In creating marriage, God did more than establish the relationship that could fulfill God's call to subdue the earth; He created the warring mechanism to keep Satan in his defeated state. And while the church is the entire body of believers united in Christ, a husband and wife united in His name is its most basic form.

Is it true that marriage is under attack today? Yes. Satan wants to bust up what God set up. But there's a more important truth—marriage was *made* for the attack. God put His enemy and His image-bearers in the same place for this very reason.

Satan knows the only way he can win is if he can get a husband and wife to fight against each other rather than alongside one another against him. But if we recognize that we were created for a fight and that our marriage is the weapon that will keep Satan defeated, we won't run from the battle. Instead, we'll run *to* it, and fight it together.

There's a closeness with your spouse that you will only experience when you enter this battle together. It's not a physical fight, but a spiritual one aimed at demolishing thoughts and ideas that set themselves up against God's best for you and your relationship.

Fortunately, the story of the Fall didn't end in the Garden of Eden. It didn't end with brokenness and shame, guilt and blame.

It ended at the cross.

Jesus lived a sinless life, died a perfect death, went down into Hell, and snatched man's God-given authority out of Satan's hand.

And now, He gives it back to us! It's our responsibility to walk in that authority and keep Satan a defeated foe—to use his attacks to strengthen us rather than separate us, to turn conflict and quarrels into passion and purpose by choosing to fight alongside each other as allies rather than against each other as enemies.

When we do this, we win. Satan loses.

The kingdom of light overcomes the kingdom of darkness.

And God gave us the gift of marriage to do just that.

KEY TAKEAWAY:

Your marriage was made for a fight. God designed you and your spouse to be the warring mechanism to keep Satan in his defeated state. He attacks you *personally* to separate you *relationally*. But God gives you His authority to fight and win. And when you do, you'll discover the beauty in battle.

QUESTIONS FOR CLOSER CONNECTION. ASK EACH OTHER:

1. Have we ever truly considered the spiritual battle that's taking place when we fight?
2. Are we resolved to fight together and not let Satan win?
3. Are we committed to no longer seeing each other as enemies but as allies against Satan?

CHAPTER 6

I'M TRIGGERED

"Change your thoughts and you can change the world."
– Norman Vincent Peale

Tori:

Seeing the spiritual battle that's taking place against your marriage isn't the only thing you need to do in order to fight and win in your relationship. You also need to get your *thinking* straight! In marriage, and in every other area of life, Satan's attacks come in the form of thoughts.

Jason's dad often says, "The warfare for your soul takes place on the battlefield of your mind." There's a lot of truth packed into that little statement. Jason and I learned quickly that bad thinking leads to bad behavior, which ultimately leads to broken relationships. So, in the next three chapters we're going to focus on the power of proper thinking.

For the last several years, we've engulfed ourselves in the study of the brain and how thoughts impact behavior. It's fascinating to see how our brains operate. Recently, I sat mesmerized as a neuroscientist explained how our brains are like forests and our thoughts establish pathways inside them. It actually made sense.

I thought about the path in the forest behind our home. When we first moved into our house, it was one of the things I fell in love with. The day I stumbled upon that beautiful trail, I knew we'd hit the jackpot.

"Babe!! You're not going to believe this," I told Jason over the phone that day. "We have a hiking trail all throughout the forest out back!"

With three little ones in the house at the time, we often felt stir-crazy during that season. A hiking trail right out back gave me hope we would survive those challenging years.

One day, not long after moving in, I ventured out on the trail with my three little ducks in a row. Our new neighbor, Dave, came riding toward us on a mountain bike. The sweet, quiet man stopped to greet us. He just stood there, straddling his bike, wearing a helmet and a big smile. The silence was a little awkward.

"Isn't this trail amazing?" I asked, trying to break it. Dave chuckled a little but said nothing. He just kept smiling.

"Any idea who made it?" I asked, wondering what his voice sounded like. His wife Bonnie had done all the talking when we first met.

"Oh, I just rode my bike through here a whole bunch," he said in a soft voice that made me think of the famous painter, Bob Ross. "I think my neighbor's boy has been riding his four-wheelers over it too, so now it's wider than it used to be."

The glorious hiking trail in our backyard hadn't been created in some major outdoorsy operation, the way I had imagined. It simply started one day with Dave going for a ride in the woods and knocking down a small path with his bike's tires. Each day he rode, there was less resistance, until it became a well-established path. And now we all follow Dave's path in the woods behind our home.

A quote I have displayed on a folded white index card on my desk at home confirms this idea: "Consistency compounds."

Very much like the path Dave created in our forest, we create pathways in our brain by what we think about. The more we take the path, the better established it becomes, and the more naturally we will turn onto it again.

It only takes one powerful thought to start a pathway like this. As you continue in that pattern, it becomes easier and easier to think a certain way. These established thought paths become our go-to routes. Often, we don't even think about what we are thinking about; we just follow the path of least resistance.

The problem comes when we establish paths that lead to places we shouldn't go—places that divide us from truths that strengthen us. Satan's goal is to get you on these side paths—away from the foundation of truth—and keep you there, lost in the woods so to speak.

It only takes one trip down the wrong thought path to make it more accessible the next time. And with just a few more trips, it becomes the path of least resistance, all the while leading us to a dark, isolated place.

In time, we begin to feel powerless to take any other route or create new, healthier pathways. It seems as though we just can't help ourselves.[11]

But we *can* help ourselves.

Neuroscience says we can—and more importantly, God says we can. It's old news, really. Science is just catching up with what the Bible has said for centuries.

The Apostle Paul wrote in his letter to the believers in Rome, "Do not conform to the pattern of this world, but be transformed by the renewing of your *mind*" (Romans 12:2a emphasis added).

The world has a pattern, a way of thinking that the enemy has designed to keep us defeated. But God has given us the power to create new thought paths, ones that lead to victory and ultimately help us discover His will for our lives.

We do it through a process called *renewal.* Renewal is replacing the old with the new. When we stop at the entrance of a well-established thought path and choose a new path instead, the old route eventually becomes overgrown, while the new one becomes better and better established.

Several years into our marriage, I began to see the danger of taking the path of least resistance in my thoughts toward Jason. It was a path isolating me from my greatest ally. And I grew tired from fighting solo.

THINK HAPPY THOUGHTS

I grew up in a small town in New England. Many of the families in Torrington, Connecticut, had Italian roots. And we were proud of it, I should add. My grandfather was full-blooded Italian, and I am only one-fourth. But if you ask me what I am—I'm Italian.

My dad's grandparents were a couple of the many Italians who came "straight off the boat" to our little New England town. I like to believe it was all the Italians, including the Cantadores, who brought the *familial* spirit to Torrington. Have you ever watched the movie *My Big Fat Greek Wedding*? Italians are very much the same. Family is everything.

I grew up watching husbands and wives working together in their vocations. My parents, my friends' parents, my grandparents, my aunts and uncles—they all worked together. So naturally, when I was young and dreamed about the future, I envisioned working with my husband, building a life *together.*

Maybe we'd own a shop on the corner of Main Street like the Lambardis. Or run a gas station like my best friend's family, the Milos. We could be in some type of vocational ministry together like my parents and grandparents. Or maybe start a home-improvement business like my aunt and uncle did when they got married. It didn't really matter what it was, as long as it was together.

When I was a kid, I'd sit at the oversized desk Mom and Dad bought me for Christmas, pretending to sign checks while speaking on the phone with a customer. Seriously, I would do it for hours. All the while, I pictured that my *husband* was ever so near. (With whom, I might add, full-blown imaginary conversations took place often.) He was one handsome guy!

Well, the handsome husband came sooner than I expected, which was even better than I'd imagined. The beginning of a dream fulfilled.

Babies one, two, and three followed along quickly … almost faster than we could count. And number four didn't take long to follow. We had hoped to have at least a year before we got pregnant, but five months was all we got. It only took a second for the surprise on my face to turn into a smile as I stared down at those two lines, confirming each new baby was on the way. After all, kids were a part of my dream too. Another dream fulfilled. I was on a roll.

When Jason and his twin brother, David, started a business together during our season of being fruitful and multiplying, I was thrilled. Diapers don't pay for themselves and finances were tight. Besides, my hands were over-full at home and I didn't have space in my brain for anything more. So, my dream of working alongside Jason in another capacity was forgotten for a while.

Until it wasn't.

By the time our fourth baby arrived, Jason was traveling a lot building his business. That was when my heart began to remember what I had always hoped would be.

Conversations during those trips went something like this:

Jason (in an overly excited tone): "Hey, Babe! We just finished up lunch at a local steakhouse—a big ol' group of us. It was amazing. The steak was really good—I'd say a nine! (Jason has a rating log on his phone of all the best steaks nationwide—true story.) You would've loved the green beans. I made some

great connections too! You'd really like so-and-so—
great people. David and I are pumped!"

Me (less enthused): "Wow, that sounds amazing, Babe.
I'm having macaroni and cheese with the kids. I've
been buying the organic kind with less sodium, but
the kids aren't loving it. And Trae just put a handful in
Jake's hair!! When are you coming home?"

I wasn't loving it, either. But it wasn't just the mac-and-
cheese that was off.

I didn't fully realize what was going on in my heart at that
time, when life seemed to demand that I *just keep going.* Home-
schooling the kids during the day and keeping up with all their
activities without Jason in the evenings was a grind, but transi-
tioning from a co-parenting to single-parenting approach was
the greatest challenge. When he was gone, that's exactly what I
was: A single parent.

But when he'd get home, the transition from "be strong
and keep moving" to "let up and share the load" was almost as
difficult for me to navigate. It wasn't just the physical exhaustion
taking a toll on me, but the emotional exhaustion as well. My
heart ached, knowing Jason was experiencing new and exciting
things without me.

I would ask him questions like, "Who all was there? Any
women? Were any of them attractive? Was it fun? What did you
eat?"

I had a lot of misplaced anxiety when he traveled and didn't
quite know why I felt so unsettled. I tried to "be there" without
being there. But doing it with a phone awkwardly sandwiched
between my shoulder and ear while changing a diaper or herding
kids to the next activity felt less than ideal.

Honestly, it just plain hurt. I had assumed new adventures
in life would be done *together*—we'd build new relationships as
a couple. *Isn't that the way it should be?* I asked God many times.

It didn't seem right that he was experiencing and building *anything* without me. But at the same time, I knew it was impossible to be part of anything that would take me away from home; my heart was there with the kids. But each time he left, it felt as if Jason took a piece of it every time. A very tender piece.

I felt vulnerable, and I didn't like it.

I would interpret Jason's upbeat, excited-for-life voice as meaning he was perfectly fine without me, highlighting how completely *not* fine I was without him.

Stop needing him so much! I told myself. Needing him is painful and it's not keeping him home, so what's the point? I just need to be strong and capable on my own.

I put up a wall to protect myself from hurting so bad.

When Jason came home, I'd be cold and distant. This became my habitual response to him being away. I knew in my heart I was creating a wedge between us, but I couldn't seem to help myself.

I had plenty of conversations with God about the matter. I talked to Jason a lot, too. I struggled to put into words what was wrong and the bad habits I had developed to deal with the constant struggle.

After reading a quote from Dr. John Gottman, a leading voice in marriage research, one afternoon, I began to recognize the foundation of my feelings. He wrote: "Unrealized life dreams are at the core of every gridlocked conflict."[12]

As I looked back on my childhood, I realized my dreams were not about what *I* would be doing when I grew up, but what *we* would be doing. Jason was doing so much without me that it felt like an unrealized dream every time I watched him go. Erecting a wall was my way of protecting myself from the hurt. And behind that wall, I had established a path of thinking that was driving me further and further from Jason.

One morning, as I lay in bed hoping the kids would somehow miraculously sleep till noon, I talked to God about my situation. I knew my way of handling Jason's absence—the thoughts I was having about him and the lack of contentment I felt—was clearly hurting our marriage. But I didn't know what to do.

Is it really too much to ask? I asked. I just want to do life together with my husband.

God's response was short and simple:

Trust Me.

He'd said it before and I wanted to trust Him. I really did. But my mind and flesh resisted. I felt like the father who asked Jesus to heal his son and Jesus told him anything is possible for those who believe. To which the father responded, "I do believe, help me overcome my unbelief!" (Mark 9:24)

I do trust You. Please help me with my disbelief! This became my cry.

In those moments of crying out to God, He began to remind me of all the times my trust in Him intersected with His trustworthiness. He reminded me of the many blessings that came from those encounters, and that the way to overcome challenges where I *lacked* trust was by remembering my past victories *that included* it.

This pathway of thinking was far from established and the resistance to embarking on a new direction was strong. But I was determined to fight for it. I knew this was a personal battle I had to win.

Thankfully, I realized I wasn't alone. I opened the door enough for Jason to jump into the battle with me. Over the next several months, we talked through it a lot. It seemed like every time we had a spare minute away from the kids, we'd talk about what I felt and why I felt it and how Jason could help me through it. (*Jason:* One of the first things I learned was that I had to stop bragging about my epic steak dinners while Tori was home crushing mac-and-cheese with the kids!)

We talked about how I had established an unhealthy pathway of thinking—thoughts that were rooted in fear and had become the path of least resistance. And how every time he left town, I felt triggered into another emotional episode.

Together, we began to surrender the situation to God. And as we did, He gave us a plan to fight through it. We applied this strategy in our own relationship and have shared it with hundreds of couples since:

Recognize. Renounce. Replace.

This threefold concept comes from Matthew 4 when Jesus was tempted in the wilderness. Jason will dive deeper into each of these in chapter nine. But for me, these three steps helped me plow a new path of thinking so that I no longer conformed to my old pattern but transformed my outlook by renewing my mind.

I would *recognize* the fear triggers that drew me to the entrance of that old path every time Jason went out of town. Now I knew where it led—and I didn't want to go there anymore.

So, I would *renounce* the lie behind that fear and declare that I was not choosing that path.

And then I would *replace* the lies with truth each time I could feel the inner struggle between my flesh and spirit. Fortunately, my spirit began to win more and more of the battles as I fully committed to fighting them.

And a fight it was, let me tell you. Like giving up sugar after the holidays. I craved the familiar path.

Laying down my dream and trusting God with the results felt like giving up on something really good, something I felt all along He wanted me to have. But I knew I needed to trust Him to give it to me in His perfect way and time, if at all.

I remember one particular morning when, right in the middle of homeschooling, God revealed with more clarity the root of my faulty thinking. Jason had been away for several days and the calendar with his travel schedule felt too overwhelming to face.

He called me as I sat on the popsicle-stained couch on our

back porch. I could hear a lot of voices and laughter in the background. He sounded upbeat and happy. I felt all those familiar emotions I thought I had defeated as my mind began to drift toward my old pattern of thinking.

I told the kids to take a break from school and run around a bit.

Then I broke into tears.

"Are you okay?" Jason asked after I suddenly went silent.

I couldn't catch my breath.

"I just don't think it's very nice of God," I said finally.

Jason tried to console me, but I interrupted him.

"I didn't even dream that big," I continued. "It wasn't even a selfish dream. It wasn't too much to ask. I just wanted to do life with you. It just seems kinda mean that God wouldn't let me have it."

The screams of the kids chasing each other through the backyard got closer and closer, so I wiped my face and tried to pull myself together as Jason and I agreed to finish the conversation later.

Suddenly, I caught a glimpse of the four mini *Jasons-and-Toris* running wild around me. And five simple yet profound words fell gently on my heart:

Live the dream you're in.

My heart was so preoccupied with the dream I was missing that I was missing the dream I was in: The dream of being a mother. A dream unfolding right there before me.

"... and the truth will set you free."

The moment I *recognized* the thing that triggered the discontent in my heart, I *renounced* the lie that God was unkind and untrustworthy, and I *replaced* it with the truth that there was a dream before me in which I had the chance to fully live.

With that, a new path was made. And the more I redirected my steps from the old to the new, the more accessible it became the next time Jason left town. God used these steps to create a new pathway of thinking for me. While taking the first steps on this new path of thinking is certainly not easy, I promise you these truths are powerful and well worth the struggle.

To this day, when Jason travels, certain triggers can put me at the head of that old path. But the more I walk through these steps—recognize, renounce, replace—the less powerful the pull to go down the other path has become.

Here's the best news of all: winning this battle personally has helped me and Jason grow closer relationally. When Jason chose to fight alongside me, it drew us closer to each other. I had to win the battle in my mind on my own, but he was right there with me and for me, encouraging me to keep fighting through it.

We learned once again that fighting together draws you together.

And on the days that are a little extra tough, I know I have another option. I can just step out into the backyard and take a nice brisk walk on Dave's mountain bike trail. A well-established path.

KEY TAKEAWAY:

The warfare for your soul takes place on the battleground of your mind. If you want to change your life and marriage you have to change the way you *think* about it. When you *recognize, renounce,* and *replace* the lies of the devil with the truth you can change old thought patterns into new ones and experience breakthrough in your relationship.

QUESTIONS FOR CLOSER CONNECTION:

(The following questions are for self-reflection.)

1. What are the paths of least resistance in my mind that I have allowed myself to develop toward my spouse?
2. Does it separate me from my spouse or draw me close?
3. What is at stake if I continue down this path?
4. Am I willing to use the three-step plan to change this?

CHAPTER 7

CANDLELIGHT CHAOS

"Know first who you are. And then adorn yourself accordingly."
– Epictetus

Tori:

A question we often get asked is, "What's the one piece of advice you'd give that will help our marriage more than anything?" Of course, there's no "one thing" that will help you relationally—the more the merrier! But typically, Jason will respond, "When you get married you gain a brand new identity, but it takes time to learn how to *think* in terms of your new identity. You have to move from thinking of *me* to thinking of *us*. If you can learn to think like married people and no longer two singles, you will be well on your way to a good marriage."

Jason is the one who usually gives this advice because, for him, this was one of the hardest lessons he had to learn. I always knew one of his strengths was his fiercely independent spirit, and as a girl head-over-heels in love, I didn't even know there was a downside to that. But the whole "think in terms of *us*" advice is something that sure would have helped us early on.

As soon as we got home from our honeymoon, we packed a

small U-Haul truck half full with our few belongings and headed to Atlanta, where Jason had secured work for us at The John Maxwell Leadership Group. I would be a product sales rep and Jason would be selling leadership events. We were excited to start real life together.

Well, life got real! Fast! Jason was clean, organized, and very particular about how our new studio apartment looked. (Apparently, there is a place for everything and for everything, there is a place.) I, on the other hand, firmly believed that as long as my clothes made it into the closet—whether they were draped on the door or lying on the floor—all was well.

And then there was getting to work together on time. Jason was obsessed with punctuality, but my mindset was that if he wanted me to be on time to work, there was no chance everything would find its orderly place. I just couldn't seem to figure the two out simultaneously.

Either way, Jason was frustrated … and I was defensive.

Jason would react from a lack of control and I would react out of guilt. Both reactions were rooted in fear. He'd try to set me straight and I'd defend myself. It was a vicious cycle that got us nowhere but mad.

About a month after moving to Atlanta, one night, I had just had it. I grabbed the keys off the counter, left the apartment, and slammed the door shut behind me. I was going to teach him a lesson.

But a different kind of fear gripped me as I walked down three dark flights of stairs to the parking lot, where I ran to my car and locked the doors. I had never driven outside of my tiny little town back in Connecticut, and I had heard many stories of big-city crimes. It was my *we're not in Kansas anymore* moment.

That was before the days of cell phones and GPS, so I felt lost before I even pulled out of the parking lot. With tears streaming down my face, I circled the large apartment complex, searching for a way out. Even that was a challenge. *I'm going to get lost, and Jason is going to be freaking out all night trying to find me,* I told myself.

That thought felt strangely satisfying—but then there was the fear of actually getting lost. So, after finally finding the exit out of the apartment complex ("complex" being the key word), I thought I might check my sense of direction and circle my way back to our apartment one time first.

After about thirty minutes of making wrong turns through the maze, I stumbled upon our apartment. Feeling less and less like the empowered woman who had stormed out, I sat in my car and waited for him to come looking for me.

An hour went by. Nothing! Two hours and still no sign of Jason as I cried, listening to random love songs that came on the radio. *Why can't he just love me like* that? I wondered. Eventually, I got out of the car and walked up the scary three flights of stairs, hoping to hear my desperate husband on the phone with police or at least friends.

I got to our door and put my ear up close. Silence.

I turned the knob, cracked the door, and peeked in. There lay Jason on the couch, mouth cocked wide open, snoring the most obnoxious snore I'd ever heard.

"Are you kidding me!?" I said, waking him abruptly. "I could be dead on the side of the road somewhere and you're up here sleeping! My dad would have been out looking for me hours ago. If I ever told him about this, he'd kill you!"

My half-asleep husband looked back at me with one eye open and the other mostly closed.

I locked the apartment door, stormed through to the bedroom, locked myself inside, and cried myself to sleep.

I didn't know it at the time, but I was tired of being locked in futile face-to-face fights with Jason. This had been an attempt to get him fighting *for* me instead.

I was trying to manipulate him to run after me, tell me how he could never live without me, and recognize that me not pushing my drawers in was nothing compared to the way I complete him. Yes, *complete.*

The movie *Jerry Maguire* had just come out. At the climax of the film, Jerry finally realizes that in spite of all the challenges in his life, Dorothy, the girlfriend he took for granted, was actually the one part he couldn't live without. He barrels through the door one evening in the most epic, cheesy love scene ever to say the three words I wanted Jason to say to me: "You complete me."

But that night, locked in my bedroom, I heard none of it.

It would take years of stupid, futile arguments like this before we'd discover there is actually a way to fight that draws us together instead of ripping us apart. It was a matter of seeing the real fight we were in—a fight we could absolutely win. But we had just begun this journey together, and we had much to learn.

A BUDDY IN BRIDESVILLE

Jason:

I know, I know. I should've gone after her. But I was so tired!

Truth is, I had a hard time adjusting to being a married man. It was much easier when all I had to think about was me!

To make matters worse, a few days after my loser-husband snoozing episode, I made one of the worst newly-married-man bonehead mistakes of all time.

Tom, a former wide receiver at LSU who worked on the same sales team as I did, asked me to go for a run with him after work. He had challenged me a few days prior to see if I could keep up with his six-minute-mile pace. I was fresh out of baseball and still had my legs under me and my ego fully intact. Knowing he was ten years older than me, I accepted the challenge.

Tori and I had been married for about a month and we were settling into life as spouses and work colleagues. I had turned down an offer from the St. Louis Cardinals a few weeks prior and was coming to grips with the reality of how much I did not enjoy sitting in a cubicle all day long. Other than the occasional temptation to scream, cry, or sprint out the back door, I took comfort in the fact that Tori was with me a few cubes down.

I walked over to Tori's cube and told her I'd be running with Tom after work. I hadn't learned the value of *asking* about these types of things yet.

"Uh, okay," she answered hesitantly. "I'm making dinner tonight, so try not to be too late."

"No problem," I said. "I should only be about an hour."

After work, Tom and I laced up our shoes and ran the two-mile loop around our office park. A quarter mile in, it felt like someone had poured boiling lava down my lungs. It was the most hellish exercise experience of my life, and I've been through some doozies. The faster Tom ran, the more I tried to keep up, and the more I kept up, the faster Tom ran. He was not going to let me beat him, and I was determined not to let him beat me.

Twelve minutes later, we collapsed on the lawn in front of the office. People pulling out of the parking lot on their way home stared at us as we wallowed on the grass next to each other. Just thinking of it still makes me miserable. I vowed right then and there—never again!

After we regained our legs about fifteen minutes later, we stretched, did some pushups and sit-ups, then called it a day.

"Hey," I said as we got ready to leave. "What are you doing for dinner?"

"Nothing," Tom said. "I'll probably grab some fast food or something."

His wife and kids lived back in Louisiana. He was a recent hire, and his family hadn't made the move yet. For the moment, he was living the bachelor life. I felt bad that he didn't have any place to go.

"Tori's making dinner," I said. "Why don't you join us?"

"I don't want to intrude," he said. "You should probably ask her first."

"Nah. She'll be fine. Tori loves cooking and always makes a ton of food. She cooks like an Italian—you'll love it."

"Are you sure?" he asked, eyebrows raised as if to say something important—something that perhaps he'd already learned in his own marriage. But I picked up on none of it!

"Positive," I answered. "Tori would love to have you over."

With that, Tom and I loaded up and drove to my apartment for dinner.

I made my way upstairs first to give Tori a solid ten-second warning before Tom appeared. (We didn't have cell phones at that point in our lives.) When I opened the door, I saw our dining table fully arranged with two place settings and a candle in the middle. Soft music was playing in the background and the lights were turned down low.

Tori had a smile on her face and a spoon in her hand. She was scooping the last bit of green beans into a bowl before she set it on the table.

"Guess what I made?" she asked, excitement written on her face. "Your favorite! Chicken cordon bleu with green beans and salad." She sounded so proud of what she had concocted.

Oh snap, I thought as my heart started to race. *I'm in big trouble.*

"Go sit down and I'll bring it out to you," she offered.

"Uh, honey," I said. "I brought Tom home for dinner."

"You did what?" she asked.

"I invited Tom over," I said. "I didn't think you'd care."

"What do you mean I wouldn't care?" she asked. "Of course I care—"

Just about that time, we heard Tom approaching.

"He's got nowhere to go," I whispered as I walked toward the door.

Tori rushed into our bedroom to gather herself.

"Hey buddy," I said. "Come on in."

"Smells incredible," Tom said. "Are you sure it's okay that I'm here?"

"Yeah, man," I responded. "Of course."

A few minutes later, Tori came back out.

"Hey, Tom," she said. "Glad you could come over." Her face had enough red in it to tell me I was in trouble.

With that, Tori and I enjoyed a nice candlelit dinner—just the two of us and my workout buddy/third wheel, Tom.

We finished dinner, talked a little bit, and then he left.

Tori walked into the kitchen and started to clean up. She didn't say a word. I cleaned off the table and then joined her in the kitchen.

After a few minutes of silence, she asked, "Why would you invite someone for dinner without even thinking to ask me first?"

"But Tom didn't have anywhere to go," I responded. "Would you rather he just eat fast food?" (My desperate attempt to push the guilt onto Tori for the boneheaded move on my part.)

"I don't mind having him over," she said. "I just want you to ask me first."

"But he doesn't have his wife here," I countered. "I didn't think it would be a big deal. I thought you'd want to help him out."

"It has nothing to do with Tom and his situation. I feel bad for him too. All I'm saying is that you can't act like you're single anymore."

In all honesty, it hadn't even crossed my mind to ask her first. Tori knew when we started dating that I was fiercely independent, but I was so love-drunk during our dating years that she never really saw the bad side to my independent nature. That night, she saw it in full bloom.

A NEW IDENTITY

My problem was not a behavior issue; it was an identity issue. I had a lot to learn about my new identity as a married person.

The truth was, the minute we said, "I do," Tori and I both

gained a new identity. Neither of us was single anymore. But it takes time for the brain to catch up with a new identity. (And it takes some people longer than others.) This is why so many young couples have problems early on. It's a process to go from thinking about *me* to thinking about *us*.

The same thing happens when you become a Christian. When you give your heart to Jesus, you change into a new person. You "become" a child of God. But it takes time for your brain to catch up with your new identity as a believer. As you spend time with God, talking and listening, you come to think in terms of who you have become. You no longer think *me* but *us* (you and God).

Marriage is a physical picture of this spiritual truth.

When Tori and I got married, I became a brand-new person at the level of my identity, but my actions hadn't caught up with it because my thinking was off. I had to learn to think about *us* rather than *me*.

This is why being on a team of some sort can be so helpful for young people in their journey of maturing into adulthood. It forces them to get outside of the *me* mindset and teaches them to think in terms of the group. They become part of something greater than themselves. They are united because they know they have a battle to fight and victory depends on working together with their fellow teammates.

The same is true in marriage. When you know you're in a battle and that your spouse is on your side, you remain united because you know your life and the life of your relationship depends on the two of you working together.

The enemy wants you to think independently of your spouse. He's fine with you thinking about yourself and not considering your partner because he knows that kind of thinking will rip your marriage apart.

We've seen this a lot with couples we've counseled. Either the husband is ambitiously building his thing while not considering the wife, or the wife is building her thing while not considering the husband. In today's "platform building" culture of social media, this problem is growing more prevalent. The solution is always for them to change their thinking from *me* to *we*.

Tim Keller, in his book *The Meaning of Marriage,* writes that the main enemy of marriage is "sinful self-centeredness." He then goes on to say your main ally in marriage is the Holy Spirit.[13]

The Holy Spirit knows how to change two people from thinking *me* to *we*—to get them thinking in terms of their new identity as a married couple. And He does it through the same process Tori used to change her negative thought patterns into positive ones (as she explained in the last chapter).

"... be transformed by the renewing of your mind" (Romans 12:2a).

The Greek word for "transform" is *metamorphoo*, where we get our word "metamorphosis." It means "a change of the form or nature of a thing or person into a completely different one, by natural or supernatural means."[14]

A great picture of this in nature is how a caterpillar transforms into a butterfly. A caterpillar carries two sets of DNA—one active and the other dormant. When it crawls into the cocoon, it goes through the process of transformation, which takes time. During this process, the caterpillar DNA dies, and the butterfly DNA comes to life. The result is an insect that once crawled on its belly transforming into one that has wings to fly.

Paul used this phrase to describe the way we "transform" our minds to match our identity in Christ. But it also applies to how we transform our minds to match our new identity in marriage.

We transform through the *renewal* of our minds. We become new people when we *think* like new people. As we said in the last chapter, renewal is the process of removing the old and replacing it with the new. For instance—when Tori changes her fingernail polish, she first has to remove the old and then apply the new. If she paints her nails before she removes the old, the result isn't very pretty, and it doesn't last long.

In taking on a new identity in marriage, we have a responsibility to remove old thoughts that no longer belong and replace them with new ones. In time, we will begin to think like the new person we've become; our brains will catch up to our identity.

The night I invited Tom over for dinner, I should have paused, thought about Tori, reminded myself that I was no longer single, and called her first. Then she could have been the one to invite Tom over the next night while we enjoyed a romantic dinner ourselves that night. To tell you the truth, I still regret missing that golden opportunity!

The funny thing is that my tendency to make decisions without first considering Tori has been something I've struggled with throughout marriage. That well-established independent pathway of thinking is easy for me to walk down. By the grace of God, I've gotten better, but not without the help of consistent renewal—not only of who I am with Tori but who I am in Christ. Each time I make the right decision in this area, I'm reminded it's not about *me*; it's about *us*.

Scripture can't put it more plainly than when Jesus stated, "a house divided against itself will fall" (Matthew 12:25). Satan knows he cannot defeat two people unified in marriage, armed for battle, and ready to fight together. But to fight together, we first have to *think* together—about *we,* not *me.* When we do this, we transform into a force to be reckoned with!

Now, do you want to come over for dinner? Tori's cooking.

Oh wait, I should probably ask her first!

KEY TAKEAWAY:

When you got married you gained a brand new identity. But you have to learn to *think* in terms of that new identity. You do this through the process of renewal where you replace your old independent thoughts of *me* with new relational thoughts of *us*. When you do this, you won't make bonehead mistakes like Jason did when I made him a nice candlelight meal!

QUESTIONS FOR CLOSER CONNECTION. ASK YOUR SPOUSE:

1. When was a time I acted independently of you and made a decision without considering you first? How did that make you feel?
2. Are there any areas where I am still behaving out of my old identity as a single person?
3. What are some ways I can do a better job of being considerate toward you?

CHAPTER 8

PUSH IN THOSE DRAWERS

*"You have been the summary of my entire existence; my
biggest weakness, my greatest strength. The weathers of my
life start and end with you. You complete me."*
– Sapan Saxena in UNNS – The Captivation

Jason:

There's a great verse in Proverbs for married couples: "Let
your wife be a fountain of blessing for you. Rejoice in the wife of
your youth ... may you always be *captivated* by her love" (Proverbs 5:18-19, emphasis added). Solomon was the writer, so his
advice comes from a husband's perspective. But the principle is
the same for wives as well. God's best for your marriage is that
you remain "captivated" by your spouse, like the quote at the
beginning of the chapter. (I think ole' Sapan may have watched
the movie *Jerry Maguire* before he penned that line!)

Captivation, as we will see, is all about *concentration*. In
the previous two chapters, we talked about the power of your
thoughts. In this chapter, we'll go one step further and talk about
the power of *intensely focused* thinking. Why is this important?
Because what you choose to concentrate on about your spouse

will either draw you toward them or push you from them—the choice is yours.

This is a lesson I learned right from the jump, and it came in the form of my own obsessive-compulsive tendencies. I've been this way my whole life. Even now, before I sit down to write each morning, I have to straighten up the room in which I sit. If a pillow is crooked on the couch or a pen is sitting on the coffee table, I've got to straighten the pillow and put the pen away before I can concentrate enough to hammer out my thoughts.

Tori alluded to this earlier, but I was a difficult person to live with early in our marriage.

As a kid, it made me great at things like vacuuming the house or mowing the lawn because my lines were perfect and I didn't miss anything. If I mowed our grass and saw one blade sticking up, I'd run over and pull it out. My brain felt like it would short-circuit if I left it there.

The same was true for my truck, my college dorm room, my baseball bag, and anything else I considered "mine." It had to be clean, tidy, and orderly if I wanted to be able to relax. My brother, David, and sister, Tracy, are the same way—possibly even worse. I once saw David pack his baseball bag after a game, neatly put all his catcher's gear in perfect order, then zip it up and stare at the bag. He looked at it like something was inside waiting to get out and he was certain to catch it when it did. Then he leaned over, unzipped the bag, turned his glove a quarter turn, and zipped it right back up.

And our sister—suffice to say that she's the one everyone calls when it's time to move. Just give her a cup of coffee and a to-do list and you will have unleashed The Kraken. Your house will be packed up and spotless before you can even rent the moving truck.

This is precisely why it was a divine arrangement for my brother and me to room with our polar opposite in college. Good ol' Tim Harrell, the most laid-back dude you'd ever meet. He didn't share our tendencies toward tidiness, and for the first few months, it took some real getting used to. David and I would have the room spotless, and then Tim would stroll in and undress while he walked around the room. A shoe kicked off over here, a sock left over there, another shoe flung God knows where, shirt draped over the back of the couch, belt dropped on the floor under the sink ... I don't think we ever found that other sock.

God knew we had sharp edges that needed to be rounded and smoothed before He plopped us into the middle of marriage. Interestingly enough, I grew to be best buddies with Tim and we ended up as roommates all four years of college. (Lucky guy. He never once had to clean up after himself.)

So, by the time I met Tori, Tim had already trained me well enough to understand that the things that used to make me want to waterboard someone were not a big deal anymore. And the first time I saw Tori's room, I realized I had met Tim's long-lost sister.

Of course, when we were dating, her messy room wasn't a big deal at all. What did I care that her closet looked like the Tasmanian Devil's cave? I thought her laid-back, spontaneous personality was cute and fun. It was the opposite of me, and it drew me to her.

But then we got married and I grew critical of the things I used to think were cute. I just couldn't figure out why she wouldn't fasten the lid on top of the orange juice bottle after she used it. Or why she left the sun visor in the car down even when it wasn't sunny. Or even worse, why on God's green earth couldn't she push in the drawers in her dresser? I even brought her into our room, pulled a drawer out, pushed it back in, then said, "See, wasn't that easy?"

(Note to newlywed husbands: that was a bad idea.) She didn't think it was funny.

Less than a year into marriage, I found myself growing more and more critical of her, which led to increased conflict in our relationship.

The more I focused on the things I didn't like about her, the more I found I was no longer captivated by her the way I once had been. The honeymoon was over and the "real me" could not hide any longer. Yes, I had learned how to accept Tim in spite of his sloppiness—*but I wasn't married to the guy.* I thought there was just no way I could live the rest of my life with a wife who didn't share my infatuation with tidiness.

Ultimately, I didn't have a *Tori* problem. I had a *Jason* problem. My focus was off.

When we were dating, all I had thought about was what was *right* with Tori. But now that we were married, I focused on what was *wrong.* When dating, I'd thought about what I wanted to *give.* But after marriage, my thoughts centered on what I wanted to *get.* I wanted to *get* our room cleaned up so I could relax! It was all about me.

The girl who once captivated every part of me now frustrated the life out of me. I didn't realize that the secret to captivation is concentration.

To be captivated is to "attract and hold the interest and attention of."[15] Tori had captivated me while dating because I concentrated on the good in her rather than the bad. But after we got married, I flipped the two and began to concentrate on the bad and not the good.

This is something that happens in a lot of marriages.

Paul the apostle gives us the secret to the type of concentration we need to draw us close to those we love: "we take *captive* every thought to make it obedient to Christ" (2 Corinthians 10:5).

This is an interesting paradox in marriage—if we want to stay captivated by our spouse, we have to take our thoughts captive. A captive in this sense is a prisoner who's locked up and under the control of the warden. The prisoner doesn't die; he's just not in control.

Satan is our adversary who makes accusations for our

agreement (we'll talk more about this later). His accusations come in the form of negative thoughts. We cannot agree with these thoughts; otherwise, we give them power over us.

When negative thoughts of Tori's "issues" entered my mind, I needed to refuse to give them the control they wanted. I needed to take them captive by locking them up and not letting them rule the roost. Practically, this meant concentrating on the good and not the bad.

Thinking positively about a person bonds you with that person. Our brains are wired for love. Anything that doesn't fall into the category of "loving thoughts" breaks down relationships and ultimately harms us.[16]

Jesus showed us this when He said, "For where your treasure is, there your heart will be also" (Matthew 6:21). We think about what we treasure, so wherever your thoughts go, your heart will follow. We can lead our hearts with the thoughts we think.

King Solomon gives us a great picture of what a fully captivated man is like in the story of his amazingly romantic relationship with his wife. He was so captivated by her that his description of what he felt makes me feel weird every time I read it. When he described what she looked like, she didn't line up with our modern idea of beauty:

"Your navel is like a round goblet ... Your belly is like a heap of wheat ... Your neck is like a tower of ivory ... Your nose is like the tower of Lebanon ..." (Song of Solomon 7:2-4 NASB).

His wife was a potbellied girl with a long neck and a massive shnoz. She didn't walk places; she waddled. But he loved her just like she was! Even more, he was captivated by her.

Listen to what he says: "The king is captivated by your [hair]. How beautiful and how delightful you are, My love, with all your charms!" (Song of Solomon 7:5-6 NASB)

Concentration leads to captivation.

God showed me that my job as a husband was to proactively think positive thoughts about Tori, to intensely focus on the things I loved about her. And the only way I could do this was by taking the negative thoughts captive—by locking them up and not letting them out.

I imagined them as literal prisoners; I would walk them into a jail cell, turn the lock, and throw away the key. I was then free to focus on what I loved about Tori. To accept her for who she was and not reject her because of who she wasn't.

But it was a real fight to get to this place because thought prisoners don't go down easy. It can be a real battle in your mind to make sure negative thoughts get locked up and stay locked up. But you'll discover the beauty in battle as you experience victory over negative thinking. As a result, the very qualities of your spouse that were once seen as threats can be viewed as assets to your relationship. I now see Tori's laid-back personality as an amazing gift to me—I can leave my workout clothes on our closet floor and I won't hear a word about it!

Here's the real beauty: when you're captivated by your spouse, the things you used to criticize become cute. I can honestly say that now when I walk into our closet and see Tori's dresser drawers wide open, I'm reminded of what I love most about her. It makes me grin to think about her frantically getting dressed for church and not thinking twice about pushing the drawers in. Isn't that crazy? Only God could transform an obsessive-compulsive punk like that. Such is the power our minds have over our emotions. I now see myself as the all-time-*drawer-pusher-inner*.

But it hasn't just worked in our marriage. We've seen the power of captivation through concentration working wonders in our relationship with our kids. Our kids are just like us. They're as squirrelly as they come, so focusing on the positive over the negative has oftentimes proven to be a real chore. Sometimes we need a little reminder, a little nudge to get us back on track. And God knows just how to do it.

POLISH PALOOZA

Tori:

I remember a time when God used our daughter Lundi to teach me the power of getting my thoughts in check and just how easy it is to concentrate my way "out of" being captivated by a girl I love so much.

It had been a long day. I was wearing down. I tried to get excited about the "fun" evening we had planned, but everything felt like so much work.

Jason was returning from a trip in a few hours, and the girls and I had tickets to *The Nutcracker.*

Kids fed ... check!

House cleaned up so Jason doesn't walk into a tornado ... check! (I had learned some lessons of my own.)

Boys situated for the night ... check!

Shower and a dress ... check!

Allie's hair ... check!

My hair ... grrr, whatever ... check!

"Lundi!!! Come here so I can do your hair," I hollered to my youngest daughter, who was five years old at the time.

No response.

"Lundi!! We are going to be late. Where are you?" I yelled.

"I'm right here, Mama," I heard from the half-bath downstairs.

I grabbed the brush and started toward the sweet little voice. But just like that, the voice turned anything but sweet. "I did something really bad, Mama." My heart sank before I even knew what she was talking about.

I don't have time for bad. My jaw clenched as I braced myself. The strong smell of fingernail polish warned me of the horrors my eyes would see next: The entire pedestal sink was covered in a rainbow of my favorite nail polishes.

I stood in shock for a moment, mesmerized by the swirl of colors. *Wow, this is actually really creative,* flitted across my brain, but was quickly replaced with, *Bad, bad, bad. This is really, really bad.*

Then I looked at the little girl standing on the toilet. The sight literally took my breath away. She hadn't used the nail polish brushes to create this masterpiece; hands clearly work best when you need to cover that much porcelain. And you might as well spread the smooth, cool stuff all over your arms while you're at it.

"Get in the tub right now," I said in a creepy low voice, trying to stay under control. She jumped off the toilet and ran upstairs, probably as scared as I was angry. I could feel the veins bulging in my neck as my head started to pound from the fumes.

I ripped off a text to Jason. "SOS! NEED NAIL POLISH REMOVER ASAP. PLEASE STOP ON WAY HOME!"

Stomp, scream, or cry? I didn't have time for any of the options as I frantically searched for nail polish remover while Allie waited in the car.

"Mom!" Lundi cried from the top of the stairs. I could tell by her voice that she was sorry for what she had done, but I was still too upset and had too much cleaning to do to talk with her at that point. After I cleaned the mess, I made my way up the stairs.

"I'm so sorry!" she repeated as I reached the top. But by the time our eyes finally met, she had no words. Just tears. Blinking them away while heaving to catch her breath like kids do when something really hurts, she stretched out her little hand with a card for me.

I recognized the card right away. It was one I had written to her on Mother's Day a while back.

Her stiff, crusty, acrylic-covered hand dropped the card into mine, and then she scurried back to the tub as if to say, "Read the card before you discipline me."

So, I did.

"Dear Lundi," my handwriting said. "Happy Mother's Day! Thank you for making my greatest dream come true by being your mom." I went on to list some of the things I love most about her, things I was thankful for and appreciated about her. My best and most loving thoughts of my littlest princess.

I broke. All the anger and frustration began to dissipate. Lundi's message was clear—Remember what you really think of me, Mama. Remember who you said that I am. Remember who I really am.

She was asking me, in the heat of the moment, to remember my *true* thoughts for her. I felt the penetrating weight of those words I had written long ago reminding me to concentrate on who she really was—reminding me that Lundi was so much more than her behavior.

I've since thought of the words of my heavenly Father: "For I know the thoughts I have for you, declares the LORD, plans to prosper you and not to harm you, plans to give you a hope and a future" (Jeremiah 29:11).

Wow! No matter what I have done, God thinks good thoughts toward me. He's captivated by me—His kid—because He concentrates on what He loves about me. Thank you, God.

Imagine if we could approach our relationships like that.

By the grace of God, because He speaks through naughty little girls, the Lundi fiasco turned into a teachable moment for both of us—a time when I remembered who Lundi was in spite of how she acted. A time when I was empowered to focus on what I loved most about her in spite of all that was bad and real in the moment.

I want to use the power of concentration for captivation, not only with my kids but with Jason as well. I want my family to know the thoughts I have for them just as God has shown His thoughts toward me. All it takes is a good dose of intense focus on what I love most about them.

And for all of you who are like me and can't seem to get that dresser drawer totally shut, I've discovered these hinges called "soft-close glides" that are now very near and dear to my heart. You're welcome!

KEY TAKEAWAY:

God wants you to remain captivated by your spouse. But the only way it will happen is if you intensely focus on what's *good* and not on what's *bad*. Concentration leads to captivation.

QUESTIONS FOR CLOSER CONNECTION.
ASK YOUR SPOUSE:

1. Do you think more about what is wrong with me than what is right? Do I make you feel like I think this way?
2. Do I act like I'm more concerned about what I can *get* from you than what I can *give*? If so, is there something specific I can do to change?
3. Are there any thoughts you've had toward me that you need to take captive? Will you commit to start today?
4. What are the great things about each other we can commit to concentrate on so that we can become captivated once again?

CHAPTER 9

DON'T BREAK MY HEART

"What makes you vulnerable makes you beautiful."
— Brene Brown

Tori:

In the movie *Beauty and the Beast,* the Beast tells Belle she can explore everything in the castle "except the west wing." Naturally, her curiosity gets the best of her and she goes exploring in the very place she was told not to go. While inside, she discovers clues about the Beast's past, a magical rose, and a room full of destroyed furniture pointing to a saddened and angry Beast unable to control his emotions.

The west wing is the epicenter of the Beast's insecurities. Thoughts of his past haunt him. But rather than deal with the reality of what happened and move toward emotional healing, he keeps this part of his life tucked away. As a result, the strength of the beast is used to hurt rather than heal. The whole story revolves around this central issue: If he would only open up and let Belle bring healing to his wounded heart by revealing his sordid past, it would unlock him to become the prince he was meant to be.

It's scary to face our vulnerabilities.

Vulnerability without trust can lead to chaos. That's what the serpent left Adam and Eve with; they discovered they were naked, and it caused them to seek the nearest bush to hide behind. Sharing your vulnerabilities is to allow yourself to be seen, to be known. It isn't easy, but your strength as a couple is only as strong as your vulnerability is deep.

The best definition of intimacy we've heard is "into me, see." Those couples who open up and allow each other to see everything are the ones who experience the beauty and power of a relationship with no secrets.

If Belle had never gone into the west wing, we never would have discovered the beauty within the Beast. He would have remained an angry animal fueled by the tragedy of his past rather than a soft-hearted and charming prince whose past ultimately changed him for the better. But he had to learn to trust her first. (Yep, I'm a mom with four kids. And yes, I'm convinced God can speak truths even through children's movies!)

Jason had his own west wing—a place buried away and locked up. Approaching that place, I felt like Belle migrating toward something that was off limits. It felt risky. But behind the locked door were clues to Jason's past that would help me understand and love him on a whole new level. And shining a light on what was inside would help Jason receive my love in return.

I'll let him take it from here.

Jason:

She picked Ryan.

That's the phrase that kept running through my mind as I quickly made my way to the bathroom in her house. I couldn't believe she actually chose him over me.

A week earlier, she had walked through the hallway of our middle school, inviting people to her birthday party. She was in the eighth grade. I was in seventh. She was a cheerleader. I was a football player. Her best friend, who was also in the eighth grade and a cheerleader, liked my brother. She liked me.

At least, I thought she did.

Everything seemed to be going so well. The previous year, David and I had joined Garland Christian Academy and were the new kids on the block. Being identical twins and athletes in a small school made it easy to stand out—and easy enough for the girls in the higher grades to take notice. (Sorry, Tor, just trying to set the stage here!) Tiffany and Angie, two seventh graders on the cheerleading squad, took particular notice. And as young sixth graders, we returned the favor. Angie liked David. Tiffany liked me.

That year, my brother and I did all the stuff you do when you have a middle-school crush—tried to sit next to them at the Friday pep rallies, talked to them under the bleachers at the varsity football games, hoped their parents would let us tag along afterward to get Braum's milkshakes, bought mums for home-coming and prayed we wouldn't stick their shoulders when we pinned the flowers to their dresses, went to birthday parties and hoped there'd be no dancing because we had no clue how to shake a leg. You get the picture.

One such party set the stage for an event that would literally mark my subconscious for years afterward—Tiffany's 14th birthday party.

All the who's-who of GCA Middle School showed up at her house for the party. Her mom had everything decked out and ready to rock. As I walked to the door, I could hear the dance music thumping. My heart sank. I think David may have dry-heaved into the bushes.

In short, our confidence stopped dead in its tracks the minute we stepped off the athletic field and onto a dance floor. The thought of gettin' our groove on was uncomfortable territory, fraught with potential humiliation.

When we walked into the house, all the girls were dancing around in the living room while the boys stood around with their hands in their pockets looking like a bunch of doorknobs. David and I instantly joined the doorknob club.

A few minutes later, our good buddy Ryan came in. He looked far more comfortable than we did at a party of this magnitude. Did he have any idea what was at stake here? If a boy tries to dance and people laugh at him, it could mark his future forever. No wife. No kids. No scholarship. No hope for anything good to happen to him ever again! Life as he knew it would be over.

Ryan walked in like he owned the place, flashed a smile in our direction, and went right over to where the girls were. They swarmed him and started laughing hysterically as he busted a few jokes, most likely aimed at the rest of us dudes standing around like toolboxes.

Before long, the girls devised a plan to get us boys more involved.

"Okay, everybody in the living room," one of the girls said.

We all marched in and got in a big circle around the room.

"All the girls come to the middle," one of them said as soft music began to play.

"We're doing something special for Tiffany's birthday," she continued. "Each girl is going to ask a boy to come to the middle and dance with her."

At that moment, David sprinted out the back door. (Not really. But I guarantee if his feet were moving as fast as his heart was beating, he could have made it to the next state by the time the party ended.) I think Josh Stanberry broke out in hives. And none of us saw Chris Paxton again for the rest of the night. Slow-dancing with a girl as a seventh-grade dude was a big deal. None of us had ever done this before.

I was standing next to Ryan, confident that Tiffany, the host of the party, would be making her way my direction at any moment. Just as the volume on the music was turned up, she started walking my way.

She put her hand out and looked right at ... Ryan.

"Will you dance with me?" she asked in a soft voice.

"Sure." He placed his hand in hers and they walked to the center of the darkened living room.

I stood there, stunned. I saw a few of my buddies' surprised expressions as Tiffany and Ryan danced together. Some of the girls looked at me as if to say, *Poor Jason. So sorry she didn't dance with you, little buddy.*

The song that played was "Look Away" by Chicago.

> *When you called me up this morning,*
> *Told me 'bout the new love you found,*
> *I said "I'm happy for ya,*
> *I'm really happy for ya ..."*

I didn't realize how fitting a song this was. In my mind, her choosing me was a done deal. I had even popped a piece of gum in my mouth to prep for the moment.

Standing alone while everyone else danced was humiliating. But I stood there like a champ, fighting back the tears.

That lasted about forty-five seconds. When I could bear it no more, I made a beeline to the hallway bathroom. As soon as I opened the door, I straight-up sobbed. What in the world had caused all this? You would have thought my mom died or something. I was completely caught off guard by my crazy emotional reaction, and had no idea why my heart hurt so bad.

I realized that night that I liked Tiffany more than she liked me. And as much as I never would have admitted it, I had given her a tiny slice of my young heart—a heart that was not ready to be given away.

Never one to show emotion in public, I quickly gathered myself, wiped my face, and walked right back out there like nothing happened. I joked around with the guys and hung out with the girls the rest of the night, giving no hint that my heart had been broken.

I never told anyone about that event. As the years passed, I tucked it away and moved on, chalking it up to young love gone wrong. No big deal. I actually forgot about it altogether later in life.

DISARMED

Fast-forward nearly twenty years. Tori and I were six years into marriage, and we found ourselves finally hitting our stride. We were doing better than ever, fully embracing our current stage of life with three young kids and thinking about having one more. Life was good.

But over and over, I found myself struggling with a lingering emotion. It wasn't a strong emotion, at least not at first. But it manifested out of the middle of nowhere and at random times. I'd literally wake up in the middle of the night with the thought that Tori might leave me, or that she'd find someone she liked better than me.

I never opened up and shared those emotions with her. But I did find myself joking with her at times. I would make unexpected statements like, "Don't ever leave me, please! You're not going to leave me, are you?"

She would always joke back, "Never!"

The crazy part is that I had felt this way when Tori and I were dating, but then it disappeared and stayed away during our first several years of marriage.

But now I could tell Tori was starting to wonder if I was being serious. One day she looked at me and asked, "You know how you joke around all the time about me leaving you?"

"Yeah …" I said, wondering where she was going.

"Is there any truth to that fear?" she asked.

"Heck, no!" I barked back, keeping my confident male persona intact. But something was brewing in my heart. I had no clue it was trying to manifest itself so I could deal with it. I felt the emotion, but I had never labeled it, so I used humor to cover it. Some men choose anger or passivity or silence to deal with their pain. I chose to joke about it.

What I felt was insecurity. It had been planted in my heart that night when Tiffany chose Ryan over me and had never been dealt with.

Fortunately, Tori picked up on it. So, she started doing what every man fears the most: prying into the west wing of my heart. She began asking a series of questions—all beginning with the word *why*—until my heart was laid wide open in front of her.

As a typical dude, this was tough for me. But the way Tori handled it disarmed my macho-man image and allowed me to actually open up. Her attitude was like, *Whatever comes out of your mouth will not hurt me and will not make me think less of you. I respect you and I'm here to help you.*

At first, I didn't think anything was wrong with me. I hadn't understood the core issue, but I trusted her when she told me that nobody jokes around that much if there's not some truth to it. So, I let her pry.

"Why do you think I'm going to leave you?" she asked.

"I don't," I quickly countered.

"Let's just say you really do," she continued. "What would make you believe that I would pick some other guy over you?"

"I don't know," I said. "Maybe it's when …" Right then, a light bulb went off in my head. "I remember a time in seventh grade …"

And that was it. I began relating to Tori the same story I just told you. That was the root cause of my insecurity. I was a thirty-two year-old man who was emotionally stuck as a thirteen-year-old boy, at least when it came to trusting that Tori would never choose someone else over me.

For the next few days, Tori helped me re-process the entire situation, completely disarming the stronghold it had on my emotional wellbeing. And for the first time, I became aware of a pathway that was established in the seventh grade that I had unconsciously been stumbling down for years. It was the first step toward healing a wound I didn't even know existed.

It was like she was a doctor performing surgery on me as the Holy Spirit supplied her with exactly the right questions to get me to open up that wounded part of myself so I could heal. (That happens in marriage. Sometimes you'll be the patient, and sometimes you'll be the assistant—and in case you're wondering, God is *always* the surgeon.)

Tori uncovered an area of emotional instability in my life that day that had been holding me back. I had gone into marriage a wounded warrior in need of healing. Although I didn't know it, Tori saw it. And God used her to restore wholeness to my heart.

> Note: What Tori took me through is a process we now teach couples in how to navigate difficult emotions and use the power of emotion to draw you close to your spouse. It involves three steps:
>
> - **Let it Out** - don't bottle-up your emotions. You have to let them out or they will literally destroy you and your relationship. (Men need this!)
> - **Let it Go** - don't hold onto past hurts or grievences. This is where foregiveness often comes into play. (See Appendix.)
> - **Let it Happen** - create an environment to feel and express emotion (through things like music, mood lighting, candles, etc). This is how you "stir up" what's inside you. (2 Timothy 1:6)

Exploiting our insecurities is one of Satan's chief tactics in tearing relationships apart. He loves nothing more than for couples to fight over things in the present because of emotions they experienced in the past.

While I still have fleeting insecurities every now and then, together we have exposed the truth of the matter so I can manage the emotion as soon as I feel it. Recognizing the root of my insecurity allowed me to admit the truth of my feelings. It was freeing, to say the least.

Tori:

I can see now that Jason struggled with the same thing many people do in marriage—a fear of rejection. This fear birthed in him as a seventh-grade boy had grown into insecurity as a man. So many husbands and wives suffer from this fear today. Because of it, they're not fully the people God intends them to be, which means their marriage will ultimately suffer. You have to be willing to ask (and answer) hard questions to get to the root and fully process suppressed emotions.

I could tell there were times when my invasive questions annoyed him, so I would pull back. It took time before Jason recognized that the pain from a past experience was affecting our marriage. But once he let me in, the pain of rejection that once gripped him became something that united us. We're stronger now because of it.

We are strongest when we are fighting side by side with nothing holding us back. We all have insecurities, but for those of us who are married, God gave us a spouse to help us overcome these fragile spaces. The healing that comes through being vulnerable with someone we trust is worth letting them in.

Jason and I dance a lot now, most often in the kitchen with our kids gagging in the background. Open about our insecurities, no secrets, and nothing off limits. Just a little country music—and every now and then, just for fun, maybe even a song by Chicago.

KEY TAKEAWAY:

Exploiting our insecurities is one of Satan's chief tactics in tearing relationships apart. But you can counteract it by opening your heart to your spouse. As scary as it may be, being vulnerable liberates you personally and magnetizes you relationally. Without it, true intimacy in your marriage is only a dream.

QUESTIONS FOR CLOSER CONNECTION.
ASK YOUR SPOUSE:

1. Are there wounds from your past that trigger painful emotions in our relationship?
2. Will you let me into that heartbreak?
3. How can I help you heal?

CHAPTER 10

FIGHTING AS ONE

"Ants, fighting together, will vanquish the lion."
– Saadi

Jason:

When I played professional baseball, I had a lot of time to myself during the day, so I decided to work toward earning a master's degree in counseling with a specialty in marriage and family relationships. I'd get up every morning, hit a little workout, and then watch videotapes on how to help people get along.

Yes, videotapes. Those were the days of VCRs with thick, rectangular VHS tapes. The only way to fast-forward was to hold down the button while the character on the screen looked like the Road Runner escaping from Wile E. Coyote.

On a few special occasions, if I hit my class goals, I'd reward myself with a matinee. For some odd reason, I enjoyed going to movies alone. I liked the smell of the popcorn when I walked into the theatre and the darkness of the room when I sat down. I'd sit at the back of the theatre in the middle of the day when everyone else was at work or school and get lost in a good story for a few hours.

I once heard a screenwriter refer to his job as "creating an opportunity for delayed consciousness."[17]I think that's the part I liked the most—the opportunity to jump into someone else's story for a bit.

But one particular movie day sticks out more than the rest. It was one of my rare off days as a minor leaguer, so I decided to sleep as late as humanly possible and then head to the local theatre for a "movie marathon." I rolled out of bed at 10 a.m., grabbed a protein bar and a little cash, and headed out.

After the first movie ended, I stood in the lobby looking at all the posters to figure out which one I'd watch next. My eyes fixed on a poster of an actor I'd never seen before but who turned out to be Russell Crowe. He was decked out in early-century battle gear and was holding a sword inside the Roman Colosseum.

"GLADIATOR," the poster read. "What we do in life echoes in eternity."

Now that looked like my kind of movie! I jumped back in line, bought a ticket, and nestled into the back row, fully poised for a little "delayed consciousness."

You know a movie has impacted you if you can remember the details of when and where you first saw it. I think Tori still remembers where she was the first time she saw *The Notebook*.

Gladiator had that effect on me. The movie, set in 180 A.D., follows the story of a heroic Roman commander named Maximus who is so beloved that the emperor, Marcus Aurelius, chooses him as his heir over his own corrupt son, Commodus. But when Aurelius dies, Commodus has Maximus's family killed and is on the hunt to kill him as well. Barely escaping with his life, Maximus is sold into slavery as a gladiator.

But Maximus isn't alone. He is surrounded by dozens of other men who are also enslaved. Their only choice in the arena is to kill others or be killed themselves in front of thousands of screaming fans—entertaining the crowd through blood sport while making the slave owners rich.

What I liked most about this movie was that it showed the heart of a true warrior—a man who doesn't want to fight but who won't back down when the fight is brought to him. A man whose sole reason for fighting is truth, justice, and honor ... and to protect the ones he loves most. To bring the evil emperor to justice, Maximus has to fight and win.

The scene I remember most involves a host of roughshod men, all recently enslaved and strangers to each other, being forced to fight their first battle in the Roman Colosseum in front of the emperor. The Colosseum is packed with the "who's who" of Rome as they gather to watch this small band of slaves get annihilated by the professional gladiators.

As the platform on which they stand slowly rises, they can hear the deafening sound of the thousands gathered to watch their certain death. They stand there, armed with swords and shields, having no clue what is about to come out of the gates in front of them. All they know is that they must fight or die.

Just before the gates open, as they stand in the middle of the arena, Maximus asks, "Have any of you ever been in the army?"

"Yes," they reply.

"Then you can help me," he says. "Whatever comes out of these gates, we've got a better chance of survival if we work together. Do you understand?"

They nod in agreement.

"If we stay together, we survive," he says.

Just then, the gates open and all hell is unleashed as beastly gladiators driving armored chariots rush out. They circle the men ferociously, like sharks circling their prey.

"Stay close!" Maximus screams as they begin to inch backward toward each other.

"Come together!" he yells as arrows start flying their way.

"Lock your shields!" They huddle together, making a barricade of protection.

A chariot with razor-sharp blades on its wheels heads right toward them.

"Hold! Hold!" he calls as the chariot barrels their way. "As one!" he cries as they lock shields and break the blade off the chariot's wheel, throwing the crowd into a frenzy.

Another chariot follows close behind.

"Divert, divert!" Maximus yells. Their wall of defense now becomes a weapon of offense as they shift position and knock the chariot over, flinging the gladiator to the ground.

This catches the crowd off guard. Commodus wears a look of confusion on his face, unaccustomed to seeing slaves defeating the professional gladiators.

At this point, Maximus and his men go on the offense.

"Single column, single column!" Maximus yells. One by one, they methodically take out each professional gladiator, using their own chariots and weapons against them. This rag-tag band of slaves working together transforms into a well-trained army on the attack and ends up winning.

Before the fight ends, the crowd changes its tune, the emperor stands confounded, and Maximus rises as a hero. Most importantly, Maximus and his men forge a tight-knit bond with each other as brothers, turning them into a formidable fighting machine.

This scene captures the heart of how couples can draw close to each other by engaging in the battle. Our fight is not physical, but spiritual. When we stick together "as one," we not only emerge victorious, but forge a tight-knit bond in the process.

Tori and I use this analogy a lot because it lays a solid foundation for couples to recognize the fight isn't something you should avoid, but something you should channel. When you recognize you're in a spiritual struggle and God has given you a spouse to fight alongside you, the battle becomes something that strengthens rather than separates.

God's way of making you one is to put you in the midst of a battle. When you fight it together, you'll discover the beauty that's only found in the midst of it: *fighting together draws you together.*

It's the same thing that happens in the military. Hundreds of young men from all walks of life and different parts of the country come together as strangers for twelve weeks of boot camp, then are sent off to a foreign battlefield. They return as a band of brothers. Fighting together draws them together because they know the only way to defeat the enemy is to fight alongside each other "as one."

THREE BATTLES

A question we often hear from couples is, "What battle?" Glad you asked!

In our own relationship and those of the couples we've counseled, we see three battles taking place:

- The *personal* battle
- The *relational* battle
- The *Kingdom* battle

The *personal* battle is our individual struggle against sin. This is the battle we all face on a daily basis where temptation comes and we either say "yes" or "no" to it. Satan attacks us individually before he separates us relationally. Sin always promises power, but only delivers bondage.

The *relational* battle is the one we fight against each other. It's the battle that takes place when we see each other as enemies and no longer allies. It's when *my* thing becomes more important than *our* thing, so we end up fighting against each other rather than alongside one another.

The *Kingdom* battle is the fight for the hearts and souls of people. It's the fight against the forces of evil that takes place as we seek to help others. We call it the "Kingdom" battle because we were created in God's image with the mandate to represent His Kingdom on the earth, and our job is to help others know Him. We are to be the bridge that connects people to God. In the Kingdom battle, we focus on *God's* thing over *my* thing and even over *our* thing.

Here's the key: the more *victorious* we are in the personal battle and the more we *stay out* of the relational battle, the more *powerful* we are in the Kingdom battle.

God has designed your relationship for His power to flow through you into the world. A marriage that is void of this power only becomes a shell of what it is intended to be. Two people experiencing personal victory over temptation and working side-by-side in an effort to build God's Kingdom is a powerful relationship.

Sometimes people ask us if two people who don't believe in God can have a good relationship. Our answer is always, "Yes, of course, they can." If they honor God's principles—like honesty, integrity, selflessness, and a desire to serve each other—they can have a *great* relationship. But while they may experience relational *health* without God, they can only experience relational *wholeness* with Him. Apart from a relationship with the God who created them, they can never be truly complete.

That's why our goal is not for you just to have a good relationship, or even a great relationship. We want you to have a *powerful* relationship—one that fulfills the Kingdom purpose for which it was designed, where your marriage makes others want to know the same God you know.

But Satan never goes down without a fight. He wants to keep you *defeated* in the personal battle, *occupied* in the relational battle, and *powerless* in the Kingdom battle. In this way, he not only keeps you captive with your own issues, but also blunts your ability to help others.

Tori:

We saw this exact scenario play out in the lives of a young couple we counseled a few years ago.

One day, we saw a young woman named Sara sitting alone in church. We thought it was odd because she and her husband, Cory, had only been married a few months and seemed to be getting along fine. But on that day, Sara sat there by herself and cried.

A few of us women in the church gathered around her and prayed. She opened up and said she and Cory had gotten into several fights, and he had recently gotten so mad that he left her and went back home to Florida to stay with his parents.

A couple guys from the church called to check on him. He admitted to leaving her but said he did it so he could have some space to think. He eventually agreed to come back and meet with the guys. Meanwhile, I reached out to Sara and invited her and Cory over to our house to meet with me and Jason.

A few days later, they were sitting on our couch a few feet from each other, clearly agitated.

"How was the ride over?" Jason asked.

"Terrible!" Sara said, sitting back abruptly with her arms folded.

I looked at Cory. "We're struggling," he admitted in a defeated tone.

"Well, I've got good news for you," Jason said, trying to lighten the mood. "The fact you guys showed up is a sign there's hope."

They didn't look too convinced. He continued, "If you're here, that tells us two things—there's something you're fighting *about* and there's something worth fighting *for*. If you keep number two in mind, you can fix number one."

We shared with them a little stat we learned from Tim Keller's book *The Meaning of Marriage*. Among couples who "fall out of love" in the first five years of marriage, two-thirds of the ones who choose to stay together end up happier than when they first married. This is because they choose to love even when they don't feel like it, and God rewards that type of effort.[18]

C.S. Lewis echoed this beautiful concept: "When you first get married," he wrote, "you have to allow your love to die, which is your emotional feeling of love. When it dies it can be raised back to life and be a much deeper, fuller love than you've ever experienced."[19]

Over the next few hours, as Sara and Cory began to unload what was bottled up in their hearts, we saw a few deep-rooted issues emerge. While Sara was dealing with issues stemming from feeling neglected and unloved by her father, Cory tended to run from his insecurities. This type of emotional match created an automatic downward spiral, because the minute conflict arose, Sara would criticize Cory, which would make him run from her, only to make her feel neglected. And since she was such a fighter, she responded by lashing out at him for neglecting her, which made him want to stay away even longer. They were caught in a vicious cycle.

Needless to say, we knew the cycle had to be broken—and fast. We prayed with them, gave them a few things to work on, and then invited them to meet with us a few more times.

The next time they came to see us, it seemed as if they had gone from bad to worse. Over the next few hours, we dug deep and uncovered a few more issues, then gave them some practical things to try.

They came to see us a few more times, but for some reason nothing we told them and nothing they tried helped their situation. And we tried *everything*! It seemed as though they were stuck in a perpetual cycle of conflict with no way out. To be honest, we didn't know how else to help them.

THEY'RE BAAAACK!

Then one day, a few months after our last meeting, they walked into church hand in hand with big smiles on their faces. They sat down on the third row and Cory put his arm around Sara while she nestled her head on his shoulder. They sat there the entire service like two teenagers who'd just started dating. Jason and I couldn't wait to find out what in the world had happened.

Right after the service, we headed their way.

"What's going on over here?" we asked the "new" couple. "It's so good to see you like this. Fill us in!"

Cory smiled as Sara clutched his arm. "We got involved in pro-life ministry," he said with a smile. "You should see Sara out there on the sidewalk in front of the abortion clinic talking to these moms. She was made for this."

"You have got to be kidding me," Jason said.

"One of the couples at church asked us to come out to the clinic just after our last counseling session with you guys," Sara said. "We didn't want to go at first, but we reluctantly agreed because so many people in the church were going. But as we stood in front of the clinic, we kept seeing cars coming and going, each one of them with a baby who was about to be killed in the building right in front of us. We couldn't stop crying. Our hearts broke."

"We knew we had to get involved," Cory said. "And the funny thing is, our relationship has been improving ever since!"

Before we could respond, Sara added, "Helping these moms has helped me see other people the way God sees them—as people who are hurt and lost in their sin, in need of our prayers, forgiveness from God, and salvation through Jesus—and has helped me love them."

There was no amount of counseling from us that would set them on the path to freedom in their relationship. What they needed was to get involved in a fight that was bigger than themselves, a *Kingdom* battle that elevated God's thing over their thing.

They found freedom and power in their relationship when they chose to fight the Kingdom battle for the lives and souls of babies and mothers affected by abortion. They now saw their personality differences as strengths for the fight rather than annoyances in their marriage.

Cory and Sara stepped onto this Kingdom battlefield as two, but they emerged "as one." It's been a few years since they sat on our couch, but to this day you'll find both of them at the busiest abortion clinic in Charlotte every Saturday. Sara offers counseling to young women who are headed toward abortion while Cory walks the sidewalk with his Bible in hand, praying for the moms and ministering to the dads. It's amazing to see how fighting together has drawn them together.

KEY TAKEAWAY:

The fight that was meant to tear you apart is the very thing that will draw you together. Remaining victorious in your personal battle with sin, free from the relational battle with your spouse, and engaged in the kingdom battle for the hearts and souls of people is God's way of drawing you close.

QUESTIONS FOR CLOSER CONNECTION.
ASK YOUR SPOUSE:

1. How are you doing in your personal battle against sin right now? Is there anything specific you need to let me in on?
2. How are we doing in our relational battle? Are we "as one"? Have we allowed ourselves to get too involved in petty skirmishes with each other?
3. What is the area to which we are jointly called to help other people?

CHAPTER 11

LET'S MIX IT UP

*"Know your enemy and know yourself and you can
fight a hundred battles without disaster."*
– Sun Tzu

Jason:

I saw a card once that said, "There are three rings in every marriage: the engagement ring, the wedding ring, and the suffering."

It's easier to love God than people. God doesn't have bad breath. He doesn't stink up the bathroom. He doesn't squeeze the toothpaste tube from the top and leave a massive blob at the bottom.

But then we read in the Bible about how "the two shall become one," and it seems God has a sense of humor. How are we supposed to have unity with the very person who can drive us crazy?

In his book *The Purpose Driven Life*, Rick Warren says there are four levels of unity: You grow close to the people you study with, share with, and serve with—but the deepest level of unity comes among those you suffer with.[20]

I know this may sound odd, but thinking about how suffering draws us together makes me think of Tori's ranger cookies. She makes these little bites of heavenly goodness—and I just can't get enough. They're basically a healthy version of chocolate chip cookies. I've been known to eat a spoonful of the dough from time to time—or twenty (no joke).

It's always a good night when I find Tori in the kitchen surrounded by all the ingredients. She throws in the almond flour, then cane sugar, a cup of oats, and a host of other things (I have no clue what) and mixes them all up. Then she adds a few eggs so everything bonds together to make a batch of pure awesomeness.

In my book *Living Among Lions,* I wrote about how we as believers are to be the chocolate chips in the cookie dough of culture—we mix in, but we don't blend in. We keep our distinct form even when the heat turns up. As individuals, when it comes to standing boldly for the Lord in a culture bent on removing Him, we need to be the chocolate chips.

As couples in marriage, however, *we need to be the dough.*

We need to bond to each other to become something together that's impossible on our own. I've never seen anyone take a spoonful of flour and eat it, or toss down a teaspoon of baking powder, or drink a capful of vanilla. Those things, on their own, taste *nizzasty.* But mix them all together and you have something special that not only nourishes the body but tastes incredible.

God takes two opposite people, puts them in close quarters, and starts mixing them up. It's not a very fun process, and at times you may want to jump out of the bowl. But if you stay in the battle, yield to the Baker, and allow the Holy Spirit to permeate your relationship, you will discover (lo and behold) that the two of you have become one. You will not only nourish others by your life together, but you will also taste great—metaphorically, of course—to the people around you.

The battle is what gives us the opportunity to blend, like what happened to the gladiator slaves in the previous chapter. This is why God created the very first couple and placed them on the earth, right where He had banished His archenemy, Satan. (Remember the genesis of this battle from chapter 5?) God has to get you into a battle for you to recognize the Holy Spirit's power to draw you together as one—otherwise you would likely choose the easier path of remaining two separate people. After all, it can be hard work to blend two completely different people together.

You could even say one of Satan's "roles" as our enemy is to draw us closer to our spouse. Of course, that's not his goal, but God turns his attempts to tear us apart into opportunities to bond us together. Only a Master Baker could concoct something that awesome!

KNOWING YOUR ENEMY

Previously, we defined what the battle looks like and how it is found on three different fronts—personal, relational, and Kingdom. Satan's goal is to defeat us in our personal battle against temptation and occupy us in a relational battle against each other to render us useless in the Kingdom battle for the hearts and souls of people.

To defeat him, you have to know who he is and how he attacks. You cannot defeat an enemy if you are unaware of him or his devious tactics. In the following sections of this chapter, we'll discuss who Satan is, how he attacks you both relationally and personally, and how you can defeat him at his own game.

A RELATIONAL ATTACK

There are three things you need to know about Satan:

- He is your *adversary*.
- He makes *accusations*.
- He wants your *agreement*.

Satan stands against you as an adversary because your marriage union reflects the image of God. He attacks you by throwing accusatory thoughts toward your spouse into your mind in hopes that you will come into agreement with him. If you agree with the accusation, you side with your adversary. And if you do this consistently, eventually your relationship will fail.

It looks something like this: I'm running late at work and I think about calling Tori to let her know I'll miss dinner. Satan seizes the opportunity and throws a thought into my mind: *She's going to be upset with me for being late. I just know it. She never cuts me any slack when I'm late. I'm just trying to provide for her and the kids. Why can't she just give me a break?* I find myself getting mad at Tori even though she hasn't done anything wrong!

Let's say I do make that call, though. Tori could then face a different accusatory thought toward me: *Jason is always late. If he really cared about the kids and me, he'd make a way to be home on time. If he doesn't care, then why should I care?! I'm not making dinner tonight. He can make it himself!*

If Tori agrees with these accusations and makes these thoughts her own, she's now sided with the adversary. By the time I get home, she might give me the silent treatment. Satan then seizes that opportunity to throw more thoughts in my mind: *She's too hard on me. I need some space from her. I think I'll go watch a game with the boys and stay away.*

See how that works? The end result is a broken relationship.

But if we see our enemy for who he is—an adversary who makes accusations for our agreement—it gives us the proper foundation we need to resist him relationally.[21]

A PERSONAL ATTACK

But Satan isn't satisfied with simply destroying your relationship; he wants to destroy *you*! When couples come to us for counsel, they typically want to talk about the relational battle, but we point them to the personal battle first because that is where the real fight takes place. You have to win *personally* if you're going to succeed *relationally*.

Going back to Genesis, we see Satan's battle strategy against you personally played out in three ways, and it's the same game plan he's used ever since.

He *distracts* us so that we focus on *my* thing over *our* thing or *God's* thing. This is where his accusatory thoughts tempt us to focus on ourselves rather than on our relationship.

He *deceives* us into believing a lie. Sin is meeting a God-given need in a God-forbidden way, so behind every temptation is a lie that promises to bring fulfillment.

He *divides* us from those we love the most. It starts with God and then filters into our marriage. When we allow ourselves to be distracted and deceived, we divide ourselves from God and our spouse. Remember when Adam accused both God and Eve when he had succumbed to temptation in the garden? "The woman *you* put here with me—*she* gave me some fruit from the tree, and I ate it" (Genesis 3:12, emphasis added). The "you" is Adam implying that it's God's fault for putting Eve there in the first place, and the "she" is throwing Eve under the bus for good measure.

This is what it looks like to side with the accuser.

Division is always the goal, because that's how relationships break. Again, Satan can't win if we remain connected to God and our spouse. It's impossible. He has to try to dismember us from each other so that we no longer have the unity of the Spirit that makes us powerful. When we are dismembered, we are no longer whole, but only a fragment of what we could and should be together.

Going back a little further in that first recorded temptation, when Satan approached Eve, his point of attack came at the level of relationship. "Did God *really* say …?" (Genesis 3:1). Essentially, *I know you and God have this relationship going, but you need to know He's keeping something from you. He knows something you should know but He doesn't want to share it with you.*

Satan got Eve to question her personal relationship with God. How did he do it?

He *distracted* her with the beauty of the fruit.

He *deceived* her into believing it was okay to eat and that God was holding out on them.

He *divided* her from God as she hid herself, and from her husband as she covered herself.[22]

Of course, there's a lot more to the story, but this pattern helps you understand in simple terms how Satan attacks.

Fast forward several thousand years to the temptation of Jesus. He fasted for forty days before Satan showed up. Notice the similarities between how Satan approached Him and how he had also approached Eve: "*If* you are the Son of God ..." (Matthew 4:3).

Satan approached Him at the level of relationship. *So, you're God's Son, huh? Then why are you so hungry? A good dad wouldn't let you starve like this.*

"Tell these stones to become bread," Satan said. *Prove yourself! Meet your need your way!*

Satan sought to *distract* Jesus from the main thing—undiluted relationship with His Father—to focus on a physical thing—his need for food. Jesus chose not to buy into Satan's lie and be *deceived*; therefore, He remained *undivided* from His Father.

Remember who Satan is. He's an adversary who makes accusations for your agreement. So, when he comes to distract you with his accusatory thoughts, you, like Jesus, can refuse to be deceived. The thoughts you may have in that moment may feel natural and have elements of truth in them, but that doesn't mean you have to agree with your adversary. Refuse to be distracted from the main thing and deceived by the wrong thing; this is how Jesus gained victory over a personal attack.

Eve lost sight of this, listened to the accuser, and it resulted in division. But it doesn't have to turn out that way for you. There is a way we can fight it—a strategy that will keep you victorious personally, connected relationally, and alive spiritually. Tori referred to it back in chapter six when she used it to overcome her negative thought patterns.

This three-step strategy has literally transformed our relationship and given us a simple process to defeat the enemy when he comes knocking on our door.

DEFEATING THE ENEMY

We discovered the pattern by studying how Jesus overcame Satan when He was tempted in the wilderness. Satan's three-step plan of attack was thwarted by Christ's three-step process for victory.

When Christ responded, "It is written: Man shall not live on bread alone, but on every word that comes from the mouth of God" (Matthew 4:4), notice three things He did that were a perfect counter to Satan's attack:

He _recognized_ the attack of the devil. This thwarted Satan's ability to _distract_ Him from the main thing—undiluted relationship with His Father.

He _renounced_ the lie behind the temptation. He was not _deceived_ into believing something that didn't line up with God's best.

He _replaced_ the lie with the truth. Armed with the truth, He remained in an un_divided_ relationship with God.

Adversary defeated. Battle over. At least for a while. Satan would eventually come back; he always does. But in that moment, Jesus was free from the attack because He fought effectively.

The Bible says Jesus went into the wilderness "full" of the Spirit. But after His victory, He walked out in the "power" of the Spirit. He went from "full" to "powerful" because he was _faithful_ in the fight (Luke 4:1). And in this power, He turned the world upside down as He fought and won the Kingdom battle for the hearts and souls of people.

This is what God wants for you in your marriage. If you let Him, God will turn Satan's attacks into opportunities for you to bond with your spouse. But you'll have to employ His strategy to win the fight.

This God-ordained strategy—*Recognize, Renounce, Replace*—turned out to be a Godsend not only for our marriage, but with our kids as well.

Tori:

As we mentioned earlier, when conflict arises, two things manifest themselves: the issue itself and your ability to handle the issue. I remember the morning when my eleven-year-old daughter showed me the secret to gaining that ability.

I was frustrated with Allie, and she was mad at me that homeschool morning. We had gone back and forth with our words but arrived nowhere good; I felt disrespected and she felt misunderstood.

"Go to your room!' I finally said. I was at a loss for how to handle the situation.

The sound of elephants stomping up the stairs echoed through the house, and then a door slammed loudly. I put my face into my hands, emotionally exhausted. Remembering I read once that you burn more calories through emotional exhaustion than exercise was the only hope I could muster. And I'm pretty sure I grabbed some comfort calories since I was burning them so well.

"Help!" I cried out to God. "Just help."

I thought about what God had showed us in our marriage about the real enemy. I knew Satan was our real adversary and that he was making accusations against each other for our agreement. I felt my spirit rise as I *recognized* the enemy's ploy to pit me and Allie against one another. Suddenly, my anger was no longer directed at my daughter, so I *renounced* the lie that she was my enemy. Then I *replaced* that lie with the truth that she and I were on the same team and needed to fight alongside each other rather than against one another.

I stomped up those stairs just like Allie had moments earlier. "Allie!" I said as I opened the door. "We bit the bait! The enemy wants to get us fighting against each other because he knows how valuable we are together. I'm not mad at you, baby girl. I'm mad at the enemy for getting in our way. You and I are on the same team. I'm not fighting against you, I'm fighting *for* you!"

Before my very eyes, I watched my daughter's hot anger break into hot tears. I could tell she was taking in what I was saying. And like me, she could now see where things went wrong.

"I'm really sorry, Mom," she said humbly.

"Me too, Sweetie." I hugged her tight.

To be honest, I wasn't expecting that response from her at all. But in that moment, by the grace of God, when Allie saw the enemy's tactic, she shifted positions. We went from fighting face to face as enemies to shoulder to shoulder as allies.

It became less about who's right and more about joining forces to dominate the real enemy who was trying to divide us. And with us both in fight mode, together, we were ready to take him out! Ha!

Conflict is tough. Emotions are strong. But Allie showed me that breakthrough happens when *both* parties can humble themselves enough to see the enemy for who he is and recognize the real battle at hand. When Allie saw that, she humbled herself and we experienced breakthrough. And I realized I was gaining a strong ally. My strong-willed child, the girl who never backs down from a fight, is a force to be reckoned. I'll take her on my team any day.

There are times in our marriage when Jason is seeing the real issue at hand, but my emotions are so elevated that I ignore the real battle. I find myself fighting to be understood, respected, cherished, or whatever it may be. But I often think of that tense homeschool morning—and if an emotional, strong-willed, eleven-year-old girl can humble herself enough to shift positions, I can too.

KEY TAKEAWAY:

Satan is our adversary who makes accusations for our agreement. His plan of attack is to distract, deceive, and divide us from our spouse. But we can defeat him when we recognize what's happening, renounce the lie, and replace it with truth. The result is a bond that's stronger after the attack than it was before.

QUESTIONS FOR CLOSER CONNECTION.
ASK YOUR SPOUSE:

1. On a scale of 1-10, how well bonded do you feel we are right now?
2. Is there a lie in which we have agreed with the accuser about each other?
3. What is one area where we each need to deploy the strategy of *recognize, renounce, replace* with each other? Let's commit to work through this together.
4. How long does it take to humble ourselves in the middle of a conflict and start fighting for one another and not against? How can we make it faster?

CHAPTER 12

BONEHEAD BASKETBALL

"A little jealousy in a relationship is good. It's nice to know that someone is afraid to lose you."
– Author Unknown

Jason:

Don't you and your spouse love the crazy questions you used to ask each other when you were young and dating? I wish Tori and I had recorded some of our conversations.

I think they sounded something like this:

Tori: If I get old and wrinkly, will you still love me?

Me: Yeah.

Tori: If my skin turned purple, would you still be attracted to me?

Me: Um, that would be weird, but yes.

Tori: If I gained four hundred pounds, would you still want to be with me?

Me: Uh, no. But we could still be friends!

Tori: That's not funny! … You're joking, right?

Me: Of course! I'd stay with you no matter what. You're my boo.

And with that, she'd snuggle up nicely under my arm and continue to sip out of my milkshake. Just about the time I thought her questions were over, she'd jump right back in.

"What would you do if you saw some guy trying to get my phone number?" she'd ask.

"I'd walk over and put my arm around you and then stare at him until he left," I'd answer, feeling my heart rate elevate at the thought.

"What if he didn't leave?" She'd raise an eyebrow and lean in expectantly, energized at the thought of me fighting for her.

"That would be the fun part," I'd respond. "I'd walk over to the dude ..." And with that, I'd be off to the races describing the things I would do to any guy who tried to make a move on my girl. Of course, she knew I was having fun with it and overindulging, but I could tell it made her feel good to know I would always be willing to fight for her affection.

On one occasion, just after Tori and I started dating, we went to one of her brother's basketball games, which just happened to be against the school her ex-boyfriend attended. I didn't know if the dude would be there or not. All I knew was that everyone in that gym would know Tori was taken ... by me.

We walked in holding hands, fingers locked tightly. My intended statement was clear: "She's mine, and if you're a dude, don't even think about talking to her." I had a heightened sense of awareness, as if a threat could be lurking around any corner. I think by the time the game was over, Tori's hand had turned purple from a lack of circulation.

Maybe it was a slight overreaction. I never even saw the guy that evening. (Lucky little man.)

Fast-forward six years to a time I found myself in another basketball gym alongside Tori ... but with a completely different reaction. We were in our second year of marriage and had one kid with the hopes of having a few more.

We lived in North Carolina, where you learn quickly that you either bleed royal blue for Duke University or light blue for the Tarheels of Chapel Hill. The parties you get invited to depend on which team you support. And when they play each other, just about the entire state tunes in for the game. I once saw a kid wearing a light blue shirt that said, "PUKE!" That pretty much sums up the rivalry.

A lot of people don't know that when David (my twin) and I were kids, basketball, not baseball, was our first love. But in high school we had one big problem—we couldn't seem to finish a game without fouling out. We were way too aggressive on the court, like two Rottweilers fighting over a bone. But our basketball dreams were short-lived as we stopped playing to focus solely on baseball in college.

My love for the game, however, remained strong well into marriage. Fortunately, Tori's family is big on basketball, too, so we vowed to raise our kids to love the game as much as we do.

On that day in the gym, I was hosting a three-on-three tournament as an outreach for our local community. I advertised it as "Concord Hoop-It-Up—the best basketball tournament in the city." A local business sponsored it, so we offered free food as well as a good-sized cash prize to the winner. I even called in the big dog for help—Tori's dad, who specializes in bringing order to chaos as headmaster of a private school. He ran the event so I could play.

More than a hundred guys showed up. David and I teamed up with a buddy, but our athletic ability wasn't enough to overcome some of the studs who showed up that day. I failed to win my own tournament!

But what I remember most about that day was not the epic basketball, the dunk contest, or even the message I shared during lunch. What I remember most was something that happened off the court.

Tori's dad walked up to me after one of my games and said, "Hey, do you see that guy over there?" He pointed toward a guy standing across the court.

"Yes, Sir, I see him. He's a nice dude." I remembered I had spoken with him earlier that morning.

"No, he's not," her dad responded. "He's a flirt. He keeps walking over to Tori and talking to her. I don't like the way he looks at her. You might want to say something."

"Really?" I asked.

"Yeah," he said. "I don't like it—at all!"

For the next hour, I watched as the guy would mosey in Tori's direction and say something to her, then walk away only to return again. Tori was oblivious to the whole thing as she chased our young son around the gym. But the guy was clearly in *flirt mode.* I could see that from the way he kept looking at her.

Now was my opportunity to execute on the very thing I'd promised her I'd do when we were dating. It was my chance to walk over and set the dude straight—to let him know she was my girl and he needed to back off.

But that's not what I did.

What I did was … nothing.

Do you know why I did nothing? Because I felt nothing. The protective jealousy I once had for Tori—which I'd had so strongly when we dated—completely evaporated in our first year of marriage. It would surface a few years later in the form of my insecurity as we discussed in chapter nine. But on this day, it was long gone.

I lost my desire to fight for my wife. I was too busy fighting other "more important" things—like figuring out life after baseball, earning a living for my family, and planning a basketball tournament.

At least, that's what was on my plate that day. I was far too busy to worry about petty little things like a dude talking to my wife. Plus, I didn't think the guy had any ill intentions and maybe my father-in-law was overreacting a little.

Well, her dad wasn't having it. When he saw that I didn't plan to do anything, he went over to the guy and said, "Hey, buddy. You need to give my daughter some space!"

The dude initially laughed it off, but when he saw how serious her dad was, he didn't go near her the rest of the day.

I'm embarrassed to even write this. I can't believe I let myself go down that path. I was so busy with other things that I had begun to take Tori for granted. She was there to watch me play and ended up getting hit on by one of the players, and I didn't even *care!* Wow.

The opposite of love is not hate. The opposite of love is indifference. I had allowed myself to grow indifferent toward the girl who was supposed to be the love of my life. Sure, I still loved her. But I had lost my desire to fight for her. I lost the aggressive desire to protect our love because she was already mine.

I was certainly still aggressive on the basketball court and in my effort to build a business. That's because I was looking for a win. But in my relationship with Tori, there was nothing left to win. I had already won. At least, that's how I felt.

A few days later, I was up early and found myself thinking about what had happened. I wondered, Why didn't it bother me that this dude was trying to talk to Tori? If this had happened when we were dating, it wouldn't have been a good scene. Why don't I feel even a hint of jealousy anymore?

Something was missing.

GOOD OL' ABE

Looking back on it now, the situation reminds me of a story in the Bible, when Abraham lied to the king of Egypt about Sarah, his wife, stating that she was his sister for fear that the king would kill him and take her. The king took her into his house along with all his other wives and blessed Abraham with abundant wealth as a result. (See Genesis 12:11-20.)

Although we can't fully comprehend why Abe would do such a thing, we have to remember that, back then, the king could do whatever he wanted with whomever he wanted at any time. If he desired a certain woman and she was married, he could have the husband killed and take her for himself.

Abe's plan was to pose as the brother, so not only would he stay alive but get rich at the same time. His lack of faith worked... for a while.

I wonder what Abraham must have felt during that time when his wife was in another man's house? Jealousy to protect their union must have been at the bottom of the list as he elevated *his* thing over *their* thing. His quest to build a name for himself and expand his wealth and influence seemed to have trumped his desire to fight for his bride. Interestingly enough, his son Isaac did the exact same thing a generation later.

Fortunately, Abe's Father-in-Law (God) stepped in and took care of the situation for him. He plagued the king's household until Sarah was returned to Abraham.

While my situation pales in comparison to Abe's, my apathetic nature toward protecting my union with Tori was much the same. I stopped fighting for her as I placed *my* thing above *our* thing.

We should have a jealous love for our spouse—the godly kind that's protective, not the evil kind that's envious. Without a healthy dose of jealous love, you lose your willingness to fight for what's yours. You'll never enter the battle because you won't have the desire to protect what you have. This is always a dangerous place for relationships.

To be jealous is to be fiercely protective of what's yours.[23]Healthy jealousy adds the fierceness to your relationship that will protect your bond at all costs. It's that passionate zeal that fights to keep and restore your marriage union. Once this fierceness is gone, it opens the door for someone or something else to potentially take what's yours.

This is why God is considered a jealous God. "You must worship no other gods, for the LORD, whose very name is Jealous, is a God who is jealous about his relationship with you" (Exodus 34:14 NLT).

God's very nature is passionately zealous to protect His relationship with His kids. He longs to be intimate with us, but will not tolerate competing affections.

Good jealousy draws you closer to the one you love. It protects, trusts, hopes, and cherishes. Unhealthy jealousy pulls you away from the one you love. It is possessive, suspicious, pessimistic, and angry.

Good jealousy is based on *we*.

Bad jealousy is based on *me*.

What I needed to do was rediscover my jealousy for Tori. I needed to reclaim my fierce love for her once again.

And God knew just the thing to help me get it back.

KEY TAKEAWAY:

We should have a jealous love for our spouse, just as God has a jealous love for us. Without a healthy dose of this type of love, you lose your willingness to fight for what's yours. You'll never enter the battle because you won't have the desire to protect what you have. This is always a dangerous place for relationships.

QUESTIONS FOR CLOSER CONNECTION.
ASK YOUR SPOUSE:

1. Is there anyone who has complimented or pursued you that I need to know about?
2. Would you still feel healthy jealousy over me if some other person wanted to pursue me? If not, why?
3. Have I exhibited unhealthy jealousy that's made you feel uncomfortable?
4. Have I prioritized or valued anything or anyone over you? If so, how can I fix it?

CHAPTER 13

LIVING THE DREAM

*"A dream is a microscope through which we look
at the hidden occurrences in our soul."*
– Erich Fromm

Tori:

From time to time, I pull out two letters. They're fragile, crusty, and stained brown in places. Many of the words have been smudged, making them difficult to read. I keep these two letters in a binder, with each page in an individual sheet protector.

Jason and I wrote them to each other at the very beginning of our relationship. Then we placed them in a box and buried them for two years.

When we first started dating, Jason had this crazy idea to write these letters detailing how we felt about each other, bury them in the woods, and then dig them up together if we ended up engaged.

The idea was for us to see how much our love grew from the time we started dating. I think he saw it in a movie or something. He's always been a dreamer and an activator.

So, that's what we did. He wrote a letter to me full of

everything he felt in that moment. I did the same for him. We then put them in a box and buried them in the woods behind the house where I grew up, not far from a small stream.

Several times throughout our dating years, as our relationship began to blossom, we wanted to dig up that box and read the letters, but we stayed true to our commitment.

Finally, the day came. The morning after Jason dropped to one knee and asked for my hand, we walked back to those woods with a shovel in hand and excitement in our hearts. I knew the spot well as it had become a place I went when I missed Jason most throughout our long-distance relationship. I showed him where to put the shovel. It took a few tries, but finally Jason hit that little green box, splitting it open.

On our knees, we both dug around the box with our fingers and pulled it out together. It was filled with dirt and the letters had deteriorated a good bit, but the words were still legible enough for us to read them.

I can still see us, two kids full of excitement, anticipating our life together, sitting back-to-back next to that little stream with the letters in hand. Every time I look at the worn and tattered pieces of paper, it takes me right back to that place.

I want you to know that I will always love you, whether it be the love for you as a friend or a deeper love I have yet to experience, the end of my letter read. (Jason: she was playing the "hard to get" game!)

We still laugh every time we read my "play it safe" lines.

"You mean so much to me," his letter says. "My pen is not good enough to express the thoughts I have in my mind when you walk into a room. You have a glow about you that I've never seen before ... By the time you read this we will be crazy in love."

Jason was clearly more confident our relationship would last. Jason's personality is more "all-in" than mine, so when we first started dating, I dipped my toes in the water while Jason plunged into the deep. Reading back through our letters showed

Jason putting his heart on a platter while I carefully guarded mine.

These same dynamics played out when we dated. Jason was a hopeless romantic, and letters like this to each other were a weekly event. We'd also go on walks right in the middle of the rain, have candlelit dinners in my living room, and dance under the stars to slow country music. We did everything we could to draw close and make memories at the same time.

But then we got married, and that "honeymoon period" came and went. A few years into marriage, that "loving feeling" totally disappeared for both of us. Yes, we still loved each other, but something had changed.

I was busy being a full-time mom while Jason was in the full-throttled pursuit of a career. All the while, a small crack appeared between us. Although we wouldn't have called it distance, the rift grew wider. We might have said it was the necessary "space" we needed to survive the daily rigors of married life, raising a family, and building a career.

We got along fine, but the exhilaration we had experienced while dating was long gone. The flame had not burned out; it had just cooled to a low heat. Incorporating romance into our busy life had fallen far down the priority scale, somewhere under changing diapers, folding clothes, meeting clients, and closing deals.

There were moments when I felt hurt by the shift in our relationship. But after some explosive conversations and a few meltdowns in the bathroom in those early years, I thought it was time I pulled my big girl pants up and got over it. I prayed that Jason's heart would turn back to me. Then I settled into our new norm.

That's what's supposed to happen in marriage, right? You're *supposed* to feel all "in love" at first but then expect the passion to gradually fade as time goes by. You settle into your routine where you fully comprehend each other's boundaries and agree not to cross those lines. Ultimately, if you're willing to compromise just a little bit, you'll get along just fine.

I basically resigned myself to the thought that what we were experiencing was normal. And for the first several years, that's exactly what things were like for us—normal.

But I knew something was missing. One day, I stumbled upon those crusty old letters on top of my closet shelf and showed them to Jason. We were both taken back by how things had changed.

Jason:

Rereading those letters was a defining moment in my life. I was actually shocked by how much my heart for Tori had changed. Ever since that basketball-court incident, my heart had been unsettled. I began to think deeply about why I had lost my protective jealousy and what that meant for our relationship. I *wanted to want* a better relationship, but the true desire just wasn't there. What was wrong with me?

The more I thought about it, the more my mind went back to what things had been like when we dated, when I couldn't stop thinking about her, when every time I did my heart felt like it was on fire.

I wanted that "loving feeling" back.

My brother and I were in the middle of building our business, spending long hours each day at work, so I began to spend the early morning hours on my knees asking for God's guidance and direction. The closer I drew to the Lord during those quiet mornings, the more He put Tori on my heart.

I started to think about where we were in our relationship, and how that lined up with the life I had envisioned before we got married. I thought about all my grandiose ideas of life together and what it would be like when we got married, only to compare it to what our marriage had actually become.

The more time I spent with God alone, the more I felt

convicted that, while I was pursuing excellence in my business, I had settled for mediocrity in my marriage. I wasn't building my marriage "with all my heart" like I was building my company.

Just about every morning, I ate a conviction sandwich from God on the subject. I prayed, "God, bless and protect my business and my family," and God kept responding, *What about you and your wife?*

On one of those mornings, I felt strongly that God wanted me to start praying over Tori. So, I began waking even earlier each morning, while it was still dark, to kneel beside our bed. I'd put my hands on her and pray over her. (I made sure to place my hands above the shoulders so she didn't think I was trying to make an early-morning move!)

"Lord, please reignite my heart for my wife," I'd pray. "Give us back the spark we once had."

I asked God to help me feel for her the way I used to, like He wanted me to. I asked Him to show me where I had gone wrong and why we had settled into a "normal" relationship in the first place.

I still *felt* nothing at this time. But I wanted to. So, I kept praying over her every morning. Two weeks later, God answered—but in a way I never saw coming.

We were hanging out at a party with a bunch of friends, and I lost track of Tori. This wasn't abnormal for us, as I always tended to gravitate to "dude talk" at get-togethers while she hung out with the ladies. But for some reason this time, when I realized she was gone, I went looking.

I looked everywhere for her, and finally found her in the kitchen standing uncomfortably close to a guy I had never met. I instantly felt a twinge of protective jealousy come over me, like a swarm of fighter pilots engaging the enemy. I hadn't felt jealous of her in a long time, but the feeling returned in that instant—not just a trickle, but a flood.

I stopped dead in my tracks and just stared at the two of them as they were lost in conversation. Tori had a glow on her face that I hadn't seen in years, like the one I used to see when she was around me. Then I saw something I'll never forget: the guy pulled her in close for a hug, while she turned toward him and returned the gesture. I watched in horror as they held each other in the middle of that kitchen, clueless that I was standing right there.

Words cannot describe what I felt in that moment as I watched them embrace each other. A hot sensation washed over me, like someone had just dumped boiling water on my chest. My whole body burned. My heart started beating uncontrollably as I broke out in a full-throttle sprint toward this soon-to-be dead man. I jumped over the kitchen island, scattering cups and dishes and food all over the floor. Just before I threw my fist into his jaw…

… I woke up.

It was a dream. No, it was a full-on nightmare!

I instantly sat up in bed, dripping with sweat, my heart about to burst out of my chest. I felt a burning anger that made me want to slap on the *Braveheart* blue face paint and go to war. I looked over at Tori. She was sound asleep, with no clue that she was in love with another man. I wanted to wake her up and scream, "How could you, you two-timing--!"

I was ready to fight. Really, I was ready to annihilate!

I jumped out of bed and closed myself in the bathroom. After splashing water on my face, my pulse was still racing. I stood in disbelief. What had I just experienced? Was it really just a dream? I wasn't sure. *Is there another guy she likes more than me?* I could feel that nauseating seventh-grade insecurity rear its ugly head. *She's going to leave me.*

I walked around the house for a few minutes, trying to calm down. As my heart rate slowly lowered, I made my way over to Tori's side of the bed, knelt down, and placed my hands on her just as I had done for the last two weeks.

It took several minutes before I could do this because I was so mad at her. There was a small part of me that wanted to choke her out right then and there. I didn't want to look at her, even though I knew it had only been a dream!

I began to pray, and as soon as I did, I heard the voice of the Lord whisper to my spirit. Actually, it was more than a whisper. It was more like a small stroke of lightning.

You stopped fighting for her, I heard. *You need to pursue her, just like you saw him do.*

Well, that's just wonderful, I thought. You want me to pursue Tori like some stranger who wanted to steal her from me?

But the more I thought about it, the more I began to see what God was saying.

The very thing I saw in my dream—how a man pursued my wife and she responded—was the point God wanted to make. I had lost my willingness to fight for her, so I naturally stopped pursuing her. This left her open to the pursuit of others. God had given me a glimpse of what could happen in real life if I didn't start pursuing her again. I needed to go after her just like that dude did—just like I had before we got married.

In that moment, I felt the same way Isaiah did when the Lord spoke to him: "Woe is me … For I am a man of unclean lips" (Isaiah 6:5). I was undone. God had given me a taste of what it felt like to be in those shoes, and I wanted, desperately, to never experience it again. God had reignited my desire for Tori by reawakening my desire to fight for her.

Tori was still sound asleep, so I continued to pray. I asked God to show me specifically what I needed to do to reignite our passion for each other and to fall in love all over again. As I prayed, I remembered a verse in Revelation where God takes issue with a particular church whose love for Him has also faded. I grabbed my Bible and flipped the pages until I found what I was looking for.

"But I have this against you, that you have abandoned the love you had at first. Remember therefore from where you have fallen, and repent and do the deeds you did at first …" (Revelation 2:4-5 ESV).

In that moment it was like God downloaded the full playbook I needed to win back Tori's heart. I instantly saw three things I needed to do:

- Remember.
- Repent.
- Redo.

I needed to *remember* what I felt for Tori when we first fell in love. I needed to *repent* of letting my love grow cold. And then I needed to *redo* the things I had done to win her heart in the first place.

I knew in that moment that I was at fault for letting my love dwindle to a low simmer, and that it was my responsibility to proactively keep it hot. The plan to make that happen was now crystal clear in my mind.

I couldn't wait for Tori to wake up! But before she did, I took some time to repent to God. I asked Him to forgive me for not treating His daughter like I promised Him I would. Then I asked Him to help me win her back.

When Tori woke up, I told her all about it. Even while relaying the story, I was ready to karate chop that dude's jugular. (Actually, I'm pretty much ready to throw down right now just thinking about it years later.)

I asked her to forgive me for pursuing my career over her, and for not treating her like I did before we got married. I told her I was responsible for allowing us to settle for mediocrity and that I would no longer accept that for our relationship. Then I made a commitment to change. I was hopeful that if I took the lead, she would follow.

DREAM LOVER

Tori:

I vividly remember the morning Jason woke me up to tell me about his dream. He's not exaggerating—he was ticked! I felt the need to interrupt him often as he retold the story to remind him it was just a *dream*.

"You were totally into the dude," Jason said, red-faced, his eyebrows lowering with intensity. "You were all laughing and having fun, like two inches from his grill."

"Babe, you know this isn't true because IT WAS A DREAM," I said. His expression was making me anxious.

This dream definitely woke Jason up—in more ways than one. And he really did start to pursue me again.

Even though I'd prayed for that years earlier, to be honest, by that time, I had given up. We had settled into a routine with the kids, and I was getting used to how we did life. For a while, I had actually forgotten about all the times I had cried out to God in our first few years of marriage and asked Him to turn Jason's heart to me again. It wasn't until Jason shared with me what He discovered in Revelation that I began to remember.

Remember. Repent. Redo.

Jason repeated that phrase over and over. But he didn't just say it. Over the next several months he actually did it. And the old Jason who had wooed my heart slowly but surely returned.

But there was still another piece to the puzzle. *Was the old Tori somewhere to be found, too?* I began to wonder.

Life had changed so much. We had three small kids and I was pretty much exhausted all the time. Jason's pursuit was great and all, but sometimes it felt like just one more thing to which I had to respond. I found myself receiving it more like pressure than love.

"What is wrong with me?" I asked God one day after Jason had texted me some really sweet words. Instead of taking it in with gratitude, I was annoyed. It had been a stressful day home-schooling the kids. My to-do list felt endless. Without much conscious thought, I took his sweet words as more being added to my list.

Am I supposed to play "girlfriend" with him today? I thought.

I knew my attitude could very well quench this new fire in Jason's heart. Without a better response from me, his pursuit would only last so long.

Remember. Repent. Redo.

God reminded me of the words He gave Jason that literally transformed him back into my boyfriend of old. I knew He was now speaking them to me.

As I sat there in my kitchen, the kids comfortably situated in the living room for a little afternoon "*Barney* break," I started to *remember*. I had cried out to the Lord to give me back the man who used to cherish me. And now God had answered that prayer.

It kind of took my breath away as I sat there and remembered those desperate prayers. Here I was, living the reality of God's faithfulness.

As my heart filled with gratitude to God, it also moved with love toward Jason. I picked up my phone and reread the texts. This time, I couldn't stop smiling.

Remember. Repent. Redo.

The more I thought about that word "remember," the more I thought about how I used to respond to Jason—the way that felt so natural, without really having to think about it at all.

I put myself back in our old house with country music blaring. I could see Jason walking over to ask me to dance. I appreciated his romantic spirit. I thought about him taking me to the mall to buy me a new outfit every so often. I appreciated his generosity. I thought about the letters he'd send me while we were apart, which I'd read over and over again. I appreciated his words of affirmation.

And that was it—my positive response to his pursuit was rooted in appreciation.

I used to appreciate the ways Jason loved and cherished me. I received his pursuit as love for me and I naturally responded with gratitude. I didn't even have to think about it. I *was* thankful, and I showed it.

Right there, sitting at the island in our kitchen, I repented for my lack of appreciation. And I thanked God for giving me a chance to redo those things I had done that had first brought us together.

By the time Jason and I put the kids to bed that night, I was ready for a slow dance in the kitchen!

PURSUIT AND PROMISE

Jason:

In the months that followed, I pursued Tori even more than I had done before. We danced to our favorite love songs, we ate candlelit dinners after the kids went to bed, we took long walks and talked about our dreams together—we did all the stuff we used to do. We even found those old buried letters and read them again.

God used that time in my life to set me straight and to show me how our engagement should have never ended at "I do." That was only the beginning. After the marriage ceremony, it was supposed to kick into high gear.

I had lost my willingness to fight for Tori, so I had called off the pursuit. Instead, I had gone in full pursuit of a career. But when I re-engaged the fight for my wife's heart and started pursuing her again, she responded.

Tori:

It isn't always easy to remain perpetually grateful for Jason and our relationship. Sometimes it feels downright impossible. But I've found that those are the times it's most important to lead with an attitude of thankfulness, not only toward him, but toward God for giving him to me.

When I think back to this turning point, I thank God that He gave Jason a crazy dream to reignite our passion. We went from fighting against each other *in* our marriage to alongside one another *for* our relationship.

We've seen far too many couples who, like us, called off their engagement the minute they said, "I do." It always results in a destructive pattern where husbands stop pursuing and wives stop responding. In time, the fiery embers of love grow cold. But it doesn't have to be that way. God is in the business of reigniting relationships.

Dr. John Gottman says the two most crucial elements in a rewarding and long-lasting romance are fondness and admiration. He found in over fifty years of study of thousands of marriages that one of the best ways to help a hurting couple is to get them to *remember* what attracted them to each other in the first place.[24]

Remember. Repent. Redo. That was God's plan for us, and it worked. Here's the beautiful thing: it will work for you too. But it requires a husband's pursuit and a wife's response to make it a reality. Neither of those are possible without a fight. The kind of fighting that draws you closer together rather than further apart.

So, fight. Get it back. It's worth it!

KEY TAKEAWAY:

Love naturally grows cold if you don't proactively keep it hot. If you remember what you felt for your spouse before you got married, repent if you let your love grow cold, and redo the things you did to win your spouse in the first place, you'll have a fire in your heart that will never fade.

QUESTIONS FOR CLOSER CONNECTION. ASK YOUR SPOUSE:

1. Have we settled for less than the best in our relationship? If so, how did we let ourselves get here?
2. What was our relationship like at its best? How can we apply the strategy of *remember, repent, redo* to get back there again?
3. What are some things I did to pursue you before we got married that you would like me to do again?

CHAPTER 14

THANK YOU, MA'AM

*"When we focus on our gratitude, the tide of disappointment
goes out, and the tide of love rushes in."*
– Kristin Armstrong

Jason:

The other day, a couple asked us what advice we would give
to help keep their marriage strong. We shared the power of fighting together and how it draws you together. But then we told
them that fighting a spiritual battle together is only as strong as
your appreciation for the person you're fighting alongside—that
they needed to cultivate a heart of *radical, proactive appreciation*
for one another.

More than anything else in our relationship, our appreciation for each other has helped strengthen our bond the most. It's
been cool to learn that brain science actually backs this up. (More
on that later.) Gratitude in relationship is so important that we're
going to spend the next two chapters talking about it.

In America, we have military appreciation days to show our
gratitude toward those who fight *for* us. In marriage, we need to

show this same appreciation toward the person who fights *alongside* us (and not just once a year).

Even when you know you're in a battle and you have a buddy who has your back, it's easy to take them for granted. The problem is, once gratitude starts to fade, love grows cold. That's where I found myself right before God gave me that dream that shook my world and woke me up.

I began to ask God every morning what I could do to fall more in love with Tori. And as I continued to remember the things I loved about her, I found myself feeling more and more thankful for her. And the more thankful I felt toward her, the more my heart was drawn to her. God was clearly guiding me through an attitude of gratitude.

Up to this point, I had been thankful for my wife, of course. But it was more a subconscious level of gratitude where I was generally thankful, not specifically so. And I certainly didn't voice it like I should have. I mean, I'd tell Tori, "Thank you for lunch," or "Thank you for picking up the kids," or "The house looks great," but I didn't show sincere appreciation for the person she was to me.

I had no clue what I was missing out on. I had not harnessed the intense power of gratitude in my relationship with Tori. I had not cultivated a frame of mind where I felt proactively thankful for specific things and voiced my appreciation to her.

I saw this power of gratitude at work in my relationship with the Lord. When I proactively thought about what I was thankful for in God, it drew my heart toward Him. I experienced firsthand in my relationship with God the magnetizing effect of gratitude. But now I had this very clear leading of the Holy Spirit to do the same thing with Tori … and I wasn't sure where to start.

One morning I got up early to try this out. As I prayed for our relationship, I began to actively think about all the good things I liked and appreciated about Tori. The longer I thought about her, the more good thoughts flooded my mind. It felt like I had turned on a water hose—thankful thoughts filled my mind and heart, and I could feel my emotions turn toward her. I could feel that magnetic pull drawing me closer and closer.

Those thoughts were there all along, but I had to turn them on and let them out. I suddenly felt so much more aware of the things I had typically taken for granted that stayed buried in my subconscious.

One morning, around 6:30 a.m., Tori rolled into the kitchen wearing her long white bathrobe. (Well, maybe "stumbled into the kitchen" is a better way of putting it. She would readily admit she's never been too fond of early mornings.)

But she was up nonetheless. Every morning, like clockwork, before the kids got up, she'd be in the kitchen getting their breakfast and lunches prepped for the day. On this particular morning, I watched her work from where I sat at the dining room table. Her hair was a mess and her eyes slightly open as she slow-blinked her way toward the cupboard to grab a mug for her early-morning bio coffee. I could hear her slippers sliding across the floor as she slowly moved along.

Empty packet in cup. Fill with insta-hot water by the sink. Stir with spoon.

Then she'd walk over to the oven as her spoon clanked against the mug. Oven set to 350 degrees. The baguettes she'd set out the night before placed in the oven. Brown bags pulled from cabinet.

Once she set everything out to make lunches for the kids, she grabbed a cast-iron frying pan and set it on the stove, added a little butter, cracked six eggs into a bowl, whipped them up, then dumped them into the pan. Just about the time I could smell the eggs scrambling, she had bread in the toaster and water in glasses. She did all of this while she cut celery sticks and laced them with peanut butter and raisins because our son Jake loves "ants on a log."

I sat there and watched in amazement, impressed with how productive she could be in such a short amount of time—especially considering that she was still half asleep. This routine was no different than anything else she had ever done before. I had just never taken the time to really and truly see it. But as I watched her, my heart filled with gratitude.

"Honey," I said as she pulled lunch meat out of the fridge, "I'm really thankful for all you do for me and the kids. You're a great woman." Then I got up to give her a hug.

"Thanks, Babe," she said. "Can you grab the mayo for me?"

I'm typically a very selfish morning person, married to my own routine. But at that moment, I was happy to help her. My thoughts toward her actually transformed my attitude in helping her.

I stayed with her in the kitchen and helped her get everything ready. When she went upstairs to get the kids out of bed, I started cleaning up.

When she came back downstairs, she took in the unexpected sight. "Wow, thanks, Babe!" she said. "That is such a huge help." She gave me a hug.

It felt good to be in *us.*

As I write this chapter, I'm sitting on the couch in our den. It's 6:42 a.m. and I can hear Tori in the kitchen, going through that whole routine again.

Every. Single. Morning. This is what I hear. I know Tori will feel uncomfortable when she reads this. She'll want me to take it out of the book because she doesn't want other women thinking she's "super mom." She would readily admit to those mornings she overslept and sent the kids out with a granola bar and some cash to buy lunch at school.

But I'm not trying to sing my wife's praises right now. I'm just mentioning things I didn't pay attention to early in our marriage. This is Tori's thing—she's great about making sure everyone is well fed. Maybe your spouse's thing is different. But

I know there is something he or she is really good at that you can focus on.

I notice Tori's morning routine now because, so many years ago, God spoke to my heart about being *proactively thankful* for her. And I've learned the best way to do that is to *just pay attention* to all the little things I would normally take for granted.

Now it's 7 a.m. and the blender is on because Allie, our seventeen-year-old, told mom she'd rather have a smoothie than oatmeal and eggs. I know if I had just spent a half hour doing all that work, I'd say, "Make your own doggone smoothie! And while you're at it, make me one too." But I'm thankful that Tori is not like me.

SHOW ME THE SCIENCE

I love how science is finally catching up with the Bible. Numerous studies have shown the power of gratitude and its impact on the brain and body. In short, what those studies show is that there are chemicals in your brain that make you *feel* something when you *think* something. And from there, they trickle through your body with cascading effects on your health that accumulate over time. And those emotions all show themselves in your relationships.

You can control these chemicals with your thoughts.[25]One of the best ways to release all the chemicals that bring healing to your body and bonding to your relationships, studies show, is by thinking thankful thoughts.

The inverse is also scientifically proven: Negative thinking actually works to destroy both your brain and your bond with your spouse. One of the chief destroyers of marriage comes from a specific negative thought pattern: *contempt.*

Contempt is feeling superior to your spouse, and it infiltrates a marriage through unchecked criticism. Over time, critical thoughts of your spouse make you feel that you are better than they are; it's a sure sign your marriage is entering dangerous territory.

It's best to check the criticism right away and use the power of gratitude to push it back. This is "taking your thoughts captive" as we talked about in chapter eight. Refuse to give negativity the ground it will be sure to take if you're not on your guard.

On that note, you might want to know the difference between criticism and complaint. A complaint uses "I" statements and is focused on behavior. A complaint says, "I feel upset that you didn't help me with the dishes. Can you help me today?"

Criticism, on the other hand, uses "you" statements and attacks identity. Criticism says, "You didn't help me with the dishes. You never help when I need you."[26]

Contempt is the result of unchecked criticism. But it also brings in the destructive element of comparison. Contempt says, "You didn't help me with the dishes. You never help when I need you. I always offer to help when you need it. What's wrong with you?"

Contempt, according to many relationship experts, is one of the leading causes of relational discord. But thankfulness will rob it of its power.

When you are thinking thankful thoughts toward your spouse, you are much more likely to offer a complaint than criticism, which keeps you from drifting toward contempt. This gets everything out in the open, releases you of the stress of bottled-up emotions, and maintains the strong bond you need. Starting a difficult conversation with "I" will go a long way to communicate love even in the midst of a struggle.

CLOSING THE LOVE LOOP

Counseling gives Tori and me opportunities to think of practical tips to help couples stay on the right track in their relationship. One of these is what we call the *Love Loop*.

Picture the Love Loop as a ring, like your wedding band, only cut in half. Half belongs to you and half to your spouse.

When your spouse does something for you (or your kids), picture them holding out their half of the ring. When you thank them for it with genuine gratitude, you bring your half to close the loop and achieve connection. The ring is whole. The more gratitude you show, the stronger the loop gets.

Unexpressed gratitude leaves the loop open; it is received as ingratitude, which communicates rejection and results in disconnection. This is where I was with Tori early in our marriage. We lacked the deeper connection we could have had if I had simply expressed my appreciation to her.

The more we practice genuine gratitude in our relationship, the closer we draw to each other. But in order for gratitude to have this bonding effect, it must be both given and received. This is a daily surrender to gratitude, where you deliberately choose to pursue things you are thankful for in your spouse; and on the flip side, you choose to receive gratitude when it's given.

I've learned to add a little RPA (radical proactive appreciation) into my day and it has transformed our relationship.

It's incredible how, on a *mental* level, you can reflect on the many reasons you feel thankful for your spouse, which leads you to respond on a *physical* level. But it ALSO accomplishes something on the *spiritual* level, because when God is in the middle of it, it enables you to stand more solidly, side by side, as you engage in the battle you have been called to fight together.

And that's just all kinds of amazing when you think about it.

KEY TAKEAWAY:

Gratitude draws you close to your spouse in ways nothing else can. It not only strengthens your relationship but it brings healing to your body at the same time. Focusing on what you're thankful for in your spouse solidifies your bond and gives you lasting connection.

QUESTIONS FOR CLOSER CONNECTION.
ASK YOUR SPOUSE:

1. On a scale of 1 to 10, how thankful do I act toward you? Is there any way I could do better?
2. Can I share five things about you I respect and appreciate?
3. Can we agree to take a challenge? For one week, let's make a list of all the things we like and appreciate about each other. Then let's meditate on them when we're alone to see how it changes the temperature of our relationship when we're together.

CHAPTER 15

LET IT COUNT

"When it comes to life the critical thing is whether you take things for granted or take them with gratitude."
– G. K. Chesterton

Tori:

We've always had a heart to help other couples. Even when we were dating, we talked about it. But then we got married and the couple who needed help most was us. Fortunately, we made it through those tough years, which reignited our passion to help others avoid the same mistakes we had made.

We were armed with a mountain of notes from when Jason earned his master's degree in Christian counseling during our dating years. During that time, even before we were married, he would send me marriage books. Often, during our long-distance phone conversations, he'd also tell me what he was learning.

I jumped right into it with notepad and pen, jotting down all the good stuff. It was so interesting and exciting. I couldn't wait to use what we were learning to help others.

When we finally started counseling couples, we soon learned that fighting together isn't the only thing that draws you close; serving together does, too. Talking marriage with other couples became therapy for our own. Often, as Jason and I sat there listening to the husband's side, then to the wife's, we felt like little birds perched up high, getting a more objective view of life.

And you know what became apparent? *We are all a whole lot alike.* We may all look different on the outside, but our hearts look overwhelmingly similar.

Before long, Jason and I noticed one cause of relational tension that shows up more than pretty much anything else: blind spots.

The morning after a late-night talk with a struggling couple, the Holy Spirit spoke very clearly to me through a passage found in Matthew 7: "... first take the plank out of your own eye, and then you will see clearly to remove the speck from your brother's eye" (Matthew 7:5).

I'd heard the verse for most of my life, but it hit me differently that morning. It's easy to look from the outside in. When you sit outside a situation, everything looks clear. But when you are actually *in it* yourself, there's always that one thing that gets in the way of seeing what you need to see most—something so big and so glaring to those looking at it from a different angle. Those are our blind spots.

What if I paused and examined my own heart every time I discerned something "obvious" in someone else's—if I pulled back the scope a bit and looked at myself with the same objective eyes? I wrote in my journal after reading the passage from Matthew that morning.

I thought about how free the couple we had spoken to the night before would become if they could just see what we saw—the thing that was creating a wedge in their relationship.

It made me wonder what blind spots were holding *me* back.

So, I tried it. When I discerned something glaring in someone else, it set off a reminder to check my heart. *Do I do that too?* I'd ask God. *What is keeping me from freedom in this area?*

Once I began this practice, I started to discover all sorts of things that were keeping me bound.

The Holy Spirit has spoken to my heart so many times by reminding me of those powerful words in Matthew. Every time I discern a "speck" in other people's eyes, I'm reminded to check the mirror in case a huge "plank" is affecting my vision too.

One time, while meeting with a couple, God graciously left me with three simple words that have brought life to my relationship with Jason. This couple was facing several high-stress situations that were taking a toll on their marriage. The wife, in particular, was at her breaking point.

"I feel like I have to be his mom," she said with her arms crossed. "We have four kids. I don't need another one." She half laughed, but it was obvious the situation wasn't funny.

"I need his help," she continued. "And another thing—he needs to spend more time with the kids. After dinner, he's no longer present with us because he's constantly on his phone for work."

"Can you understand why she feels this way?" Jason asked her husband.

"I'm mean, kinda," he said as he stared blankly at the floor. "But I'm *really* trying."

"In what ways?" Jason asked.

"Well," he said, "I wake up around 5 a.m. to have quiet time with the Lord. Then I get on my computer to try and get on top of my workday. After that, I wake up all the kids and start making them breakfast and lunches for school. Then I do devotions with them while they eat. After breakfast, I drive the younger ones to school. The older ones start a little later, so I come back for them and drop them off on my way into work. Then I go to work until five-ish …"

"Sorry, let me interrupt just a second," Jason said as he turned to the wife. "Does this sound about right?" he asked her.

"Uh-huh." She nodded in agreement.

"So, you see all this every morning, right?" Jason asked.

"Well, I'm not a morning person, so I'm in bed during that time," she said. "He's the morning person so I let him do all the morning stuff."

"Okay, keep going." Jason turned back to the husband.

"So, yeah," the husband continued. "After work, I sometimes pick something up on the way home to grill, help with dinner, and spend time with the family."

"Well," the wife interrupted, "I wouldn't say 'spending time with the family' is accurate. You check your phone every twenty minutes. You are with us, but you aren't really present."

"But the other parts," I said as I finally chimed in from my birds-eye view, "all the things he does to help in the morning and with dinner? He does all that?" I asked.

"Well, yeah," she said. "But the whole morning-routine stuff, that doesn't really count because he's always been a morning person. He loves mornings. I require more sleep than he does."

"Yes," the husband spoke up. "I am a morning person, but I feel like there are a lot of things I could do during that time to get on top of my workday, but I choose to spend it with the kids and let you sleep because I know how much you need it. And I feel like I am fully present with the kids during that time. I feel like that time with them should count."

There was a moment of silence before I jumped back in.

"Can I just say something from an outside perspective and also from one *non-morning* person to another?" I asked, smiling at the wife sitting across from me.

Her arms unfolded, her face loosened, and she smiled back. Clearly, I wasn't her problem.

"I'm the one in our home that does the bulk of the morning routine with the kids," I said. "If Jason did it all so I could sleep in, it would definitely count for something! Not because I'm better than you, but because that's so outside our norm. In marriage, it's easy to take the normal things for granted and not *let it count*."

Then Jason spoke up. "There's a great verse in Psalms that

talks about the key to gaining a man's presence," he said. 'Enter His gates with thanksgiving and His courts with praise' (Psalms 100:4). You mentioned several times you want your hubby to be present. If giving thanks and praise brings *God's* presence, I think it will bring your *husband's* too. The presence you're longing for from your husband will be yours if you give him these two things."

She nodded in agreement and admitted she needed to do better at being thankful for him and letting the little things he does count. It was refreshing to see her humility and willingness to receive advice and admit her shortcomings. Whenever a couple can get to this place, there is hope!

We spent the rest of our time working through some practical things with them. After they left, I thought about how obvious the problem seemed. *If she would just be thankful for the things he does, maybe …*

I stopped myself mid-thought and remembered what I had read in Matthew 7: "take the plank out of your own eye."

What are areas in my life where I don't "let it count"? I prayed. Lord, please give me a birds-eye view into my own heart. I don't want to miss Your presence or the presence of people I take for granted.

TAKING OUT MY PLANK

That night, Jason left to go out of town. It was a Friday night and our two teenagers had plans to go somewhere with friends. The two younger ones were outside with some neighborhood kids lost in a game outside that carried on forever.

This was a brand-new season for me. I'd homeschooled my kids for twelve years, and this was the first year they were all in school. After a decade of utilizing every moment the kids were occupied to get things done around the house, I was now getting everything done while they were in school. So, when they got home, I planned to be *all* theirs.

But that night, they were *all* gone.

I turned on a podcast I had stumbled across on Instagram. Two women were discussing the value of friendship and the beauty of time spent together. I realized I was out of my routine of seeing close friends who had homeschooled alongside me for over a decade.

I began to feel a little sorry for myself for my lack of socialization in this new season. And just like that, my focus turned to what I didn't have rather than what I did.

I once heard a pastor say, "We exaggerate the greatness of our problem to justify our fear."[27]

When is the last time I had a meaningful conversation with a friend? I wondered as I worked myself up. And 'going out for coffee' like the ladies on the podcast talked about … do friends really do that … like, regularly?

The sound of a kid hollering, "We're home," and another, "I'm starving!" pushed me out of my thought bubble for a while. But I lay in bed that night worrying if I was becoming a real loser because of my lack of socialization.

Saturday morning, I was up early driving one kid to this and another to that, counting the hours until Jason would be home. As I pulled back into our carport, my cell phone rang.

"Incoming call … Dad," lit up the screen.

"Hey, Dad," I answered.

"Good morning, Tori Garland!" he responded, using the full name he gave me, which he does often. "I just put a pot of coffee on. Come get a cup."

I opened my car door and looked over at my parents' house, eighty feet away. There stood my dad on his side porch facing me, a phone to his ear in one hand while the other did the slow wave he regularly gives me from that porch.

I put my phone in my pocket and yelled over, "Let me check on the girls. I'll be right over!"

After confirming the girls hadn't killed each other and were doing fine, I made my way across the bed of pine needles that separates our house from theirs. Just as I could smell the coffee brewing, I heard the words in my head from the day before.

Let it count!

I slowed my steps to hear it again.

Let it count!

Dad counts, my heart said.

In a season when Jason was out of town a lot and I was finding more margin in my day, God had given me a friend to talk to—someone who should totally count. My dad.

I thought of the woman who had been sitting across from Jason and me the day before. The one I'd felt a bit jealous of because she got to sleep in every morning. My heart warmed to her. I could see how easy it was to miss the gifts right in front of us. Beautiful gifts that we fail to enjoy because we just don't see them.

Let it count!

It was so loud and clear.

So, I listened.

Thank You, God, for my dad, I prayed. You are so good. You supply all my needs.

With that simple act of thanksgiving and praise, I entered God's presence as Psalm 100 says. I found what a beautiful and fulfilling place it is—a place where I lack nothing. It also drew me toward my dad as I let gratitude toward him fill my heart. And let me tell you, that was the best cup of coffee I'd had in a long time.

Oh, and that couple? They're doing great. She started writing all the things she was thankful for about her husband—the things she used to take for granted—on the mirror in their bathroom for both of them to read. When he told us about it, he couldn't stop smiling. It's a beautiful thing when you *let it count!*

KEY TAKEAWAY:

Taking your spouse for granted is a natural progression in marriage. But if you want to keep your relationship strong, you need to appreciate all the little things they do. And when your gratitude is communicated, your bond is strengthened.

QUESTIONS FOR CLOSER CONNECTION

These questions are for self-reflection:

1. What are some things my spouse does that I haven't been "letting count"? Please share them with your spouse.
2. What are some things I can do specifically to not take my spouse for granted?
3. What "dream" am I living in right now that I haven't appreciated because I've been focused on what I *don't* have, rather than what I *do*?

CHAPTER 16

LET'S HAVE A FOURTH

"Face your fears or they will climb over your back."
– Frank Herbert

Tori:

I always hoped Jason and I would have four kids. When people would ask us, "So, how many kids are you guys going to have?" we'd always respond, "Three or four." Coming from a family of six myself, I wanted to hear, "Benham, party of six," one day.

Under-promise, over-deliver—that's what Jason always says in the business world. Throwing that "three" in there gave us some wiggle room. But once I became a mother to three babies under the age of four, the thought of having a fourth made my brain short-circuit. We began to accept the reality that we might not over-deliver after all.

For me, going from juggling two babies to three was no different from juggling in general. Two, totally doable. Throw a third one in and we've got chaos.

Two were manageable. In our day-to-day life, I could still take in the moments. With two, we were playing in the shallow end together, soaking in the sun. I had one hand on each of them and everyone was safe. It wasn't always easy by any stretch, but I felt capable and confident in that role.

Then our third, Jake, was born … and it felt as if the bottom dropped out from underneath me and I was treading water in the deep end, all while frantically trying to hold onto three kids who couldn't swim yet.

I was drowning.

We recently watched a home video from that season. In it, we are all gathered in the kitchen for a "fun" pizza-making family night. Trae, four years old, asks me the same question over and over while I act as if I can't hear his voice. Allie, two, sits at the counter with her hands covered in flour and a lump of dough, irritated that something isn't working right. And Jake, six months, cries intermittently because he's just woken up and is hungry.

"Family pizza night!" You hear my voice behind the camera, desperately trying to rally everyone.

Jake grabs the raw pizza dough, intent on eating it, and I take it from him. "No, no, buddy," I tell him.

Trae asks another question, but I can't hear it because Allie is complaining loudly that the dough won't spread. Jake grabs it again.

"No, no, buddy," I say, removing the dough from his reach while helping Allie at the same time.

Jake starts to cry. Allie loses her cool.

I cave in, take the dough Jake is begging for, and slide it over to him to gnaw on. Then, in my attempt to distract Allie from her frustration, I pat some flour on her nose and laugh. It backfires.

Allie screams, jumps out of her seat, and runs into the living room to pitch an all-out temper tantrum. Apparently, she did not like flour on her nose AT ALL! Meanwhile, Jake eats the dough like a ravenous wolf and Trae sits wide-eyed, wondering if Mom heard his question or if he should try again.

I felt like such a failure so many days, but I kept going, praying I could find a rhythm. Meanwhile, I learned to *fail forward*, as Dr. John Maxwell puts it.

I watched other moms around me immediately find their stride with three. At least, that's the way it appeared from the outside. Going from two to three looked seamless for them. But not for me.

Survive. That word succinctly describes that season of my life. Jason and I had noticed that June was the fertile month in which babies one, two, and three had been conceived. The June after baby number three, I looked at Jason as if he'd turned into a werewolf. We decided a pause on having kids was necessary.

Meanwhile, Jason and I were learning a lot about ourselves. We had never known such physical exhaustion. A good night's sleep was a distant memory. When there wasn't a diaper to change or wet bed sheets to wash, our oldest was projectile vomiting in the bathroom in the middle of the night. Not because he had some kind of chronic illness—oh, no. He threw up because he would inhale his food so fast and eat so much that he literally ate himself sick. We were too busy with the other two at dinner to notice he was on his third plate!

Back then, we relished the thought of our kids only peeing on us in the night.

While the nights were long, the days often felt even longer. Jason worked extended hours getting his business up and running, so it was just me home with the kids until dinner. It's an understatement that both Jason and I were more than a little stressed. We were getting stirred up, and fear had begun to mix into our life together.

Fear is a silent destroyer. It renders you powerless to find beauty in the battle. Why? Because when you're too scared to face your fear and go all-in, you often fail to enter the battle at all. This is where we found ourselves when it came to the idea of having another baby.

"We fear what we cannot control, so we try to control that in which we fear."

I wrote that in my journal years ago and I think about it often. Stress is a part of every relationship. Fear shouldn't be. Operating out of fear will cause you to avoid the fight that can make you stronger.

For as long as I can remember, fear has been my natural bent. But I've learned that fear isn't really natural at all. Our physical bodies respond very poorly to it. As a matter of fact, all diseases are a result of dis-ease (a.k.a. fear). Fear was never meant to be part of our DNA. We are wired for love.[28]

Fear is a learned response. Thankfully, this means it can be unlearned.

Looking back on that season, the greatest mistakes Jason and I made in our relationship came from trying to control what we feared most. In life's most stressful moments, we would react in fear of what we might lose—our time, our space, our ever-loving minds. Whatever it was, reacting in fear felt natural, yet it was never a good solution.

The nature of fear is to *react* … but the nature of love is to *respond*. Fear *abuses* boundaries for control, but love *uses* boundaries for protection.

Fear demands, "How can I control this situation?"

Love asks, "What does love require of me in this situation?"

These are things we had to learn the hard way.

When the "fertile" June month returned the following year, we began to talk about the possibility of having a fourth child. We were just beginning to find a rhythm with three. All of them were potty-trained (glory!), we weren't housebound by the baby's nap schedule, and every once in a while, we could handle going out to dinner as a family without dark glances from other restaurant patrons begging us to *just leave already*.

But no. Neither Jason nor I wanted to go back to those things. And I definitely didn't want to face the sickness of pregnancy again. I had struggled through each one with headaches, nausea, and mood swings—to name a few. We wanted to avoid the fight for a fourth.

One afternoon, I walked out back where the kids were playing on the swing set. I glanced over at the tiny little shed I'd convinced Jason to turn into a playhouse for our only daughter, Allie, who was four at the time. She called it her "Wendy House." Aunt Carolyn, our close friend and neighbor who has a strong British accent, said that's what she called hers growing up (inspired by *Peter Pan*). Anything said with a British accent sounds a thousand times more magical, so that's the name that stuck.

I had outfitted the place with exciting Craigslist finds like a kids' Pottery Barn refrigerator and dishwasher, and the sweetest off-brand kitchen set. Then I frequented Goodwill until the 8x8 square shed became a cozy little home. We even hung an antique-looking black mailbox next to the door where Allie and my dad (whom the kids call "Pop") could exchange letters.

The only problem was that the sweet little home I worked so hard to make special for her was about eighty feet from our house. And Allie, much like her mama, had some fears in life to overcome. Playing in the Wendy House so far away was one of them. She'd run to get her mail from Pop, draw something for him in our kitchen, and run it back.

"Why don't you play in your Wendy House?" I asked her.

"I'm too *sthcared*," she'd say in her squeaky little voice with a slight lisp.

"There is absolutely nothing to be scared of, Baby Girl," I'd say. "You're missing out on so much fun!"

I stared at the Wendy House as I pushed the kids on the swings that afternoon. Allie had only played in it a handful of times—only when I could sit with her inside, which was next to impossible with a two-year-old boy who would love nothing more than to break all things pretty and girly.

It really is the sweetest little place, I thought as a tear ran down my cheek unexpectedly.

When Jason got home that evening, I couldn't hold back the tears. "I really don't want to be pregnant again and I can't imagine getting through it all," I said in another unexpected outburst. "But I couldn't stop staring at the Wendy House today."

I could tell I had Jason's attention. His face faded a shade and his eyebrows lowered like he does when he's thinking.

"Do you think maybe the Wendy House wasn't meant to be just for Allie after all?" I asked. "What if there is another little girl for us?"

Jason's face faded yet another shade, as if the blood had just rushed out. I think the same thing happened to me. A wave of exhaustion hit us both as we stood there contemplating the thought of doing the baby thing all over again.

Fear has a way of sucking the life out of you.

What if this fear is keeping us from something really wonderful, just like Allie's fear keeps her from enjoying her Wendy House? I wondered. This thought conflicted with another question that came on its heels. *What if I am really just afraid of regret?*

Fear also has a way of bringing confusion.

We agreed to pray about it together. Then we sought wise counsel from others.

One of our pastors stopped by that week. We told him our dilemma. "We're afraid to have another baby, but we also feel afraid not to."

He stopped us after we'd gone on for a while. "Listen, guys," he said with a smile on his face. "If you think God wants you to have another baby, have another baby. But anything done in fear is not God. He doesn't use fear to get you to do what He wants. Don't let fear push you to have a baby, and don't let fear keep you from having one. If God is prompting you to have another child, walk through it in faith. But if God is prompting you to be content where you are, be content where you are. Don't let fear drive your decision either way."

A burst of energy revived me as I received his words.

Truth has a way of restoring life.

That night, Jason and I walked next door to my parents' house. After all, they were the ones most involved in our growing family. With only eighty feet between us, there was really no place for them to hide. If *we* were going to have another little tyke, *they* would too! The season we were coming out of made me overly aware of just "how much" our family filled with little kids could be.

I wondered if Jason and I having another kid would push my parents off a cliff, or at least into another neighborhood. I was nervous to bring it up.

Finally, I mustered the courage and said, "I've been looking at the Wendy House lately, and I feel like maybe we are supposed to have one more." I began to cry again as I sat at their maple dining room table—the one at which I'd sat at for countless meals with my siblings growing up.

"But I know how involved you are in our lives, and you help so much," I continued in a full-blown, ugly-face cry. "I just don't want to be too much for you guys."

"Tori!" My mom walked over to hug me. "Are you kidding me? You guys are our greatest joy! You could have ten more kids and you would never be too much."

Dad chimed in with his Northern accent, "Ten's a little much, don't-cha think, Crick?" (Crick is his nickname for my mom.) Then he winked and smiled at me. "Come on. You're a great mom. Have another kid." He pulled me in for a hug.

Something about their loving response quieted the fear in my heart. They weren't afraid of us being too much for *them*. I could let go of the fear of another baby being too much for *us*.

Love has power over fear. I experienced it firsthand that evening.

Not long after, we were pregnant with Lundi Mae. The fear of going back to that place of fatigue and being overwhelmed was replaced with love for a new life.

Lundi is now our cherry on top. We can't imagine life

without her. We are so thankful our fear of the past didn't alter the joy of our future. Her life is a constant reminder of this.

And now we are "Benham, party of six!" Our family is stronger with her in it. Strength through strain. That's what beauty in battle is all about. But to get it, you have to bust through your fear.

Our greatest blessing is found on the other side of our greatest fear. Only when we turn and face it, and attack it with love, can we embrace the blessing on the other side. Fighting through that fear has brought such beauty, joy, and strength to our family—in the person of our little cherry on top!

KEY TAKEAWAY:

Fear is a silent destroyer. It renders you powerless to find beauty in the battle. It keeps you from going all-in. You have to face your fear before God will take over the fight. And when He does, you'll discover a relationship worth fighting for.

QUESTIONS FOR CLOSER CONNECTION.
ASK YOUR SPOUSE:

1. Is there an area where you feel like I am trying to control you out of fear right now? What can I do to set you free?
2. Is there an area where we, together, are trying to control something we fear? What kind of fruit is that bearing?
3. What can we do practically to operate more out of love than fear? For our relationship? For our kids?

CHAPTER 17

FIGHTING FOR VICTORY

"It ain't about how hard you hit; it's about how hard you can get hit and keep moving forward. It's how much you can take, and keep moving forward. That's how winning is done."
– Rocky Balboa

Tori:

We've talked a lot about the spiritual battle and how fighting it together draws you together. But what if that spiritual struggle turns physical and you find yourself in the midst of a crisis? How does that affect your relationship? Well, we were about to find out.

After we had Lundi, we thought our trial of faith was over. We had faced our fears and were experiencing the blessing on the other side. But just a few weeks into her life, we were dropped into the depths of another trial.

Fighting a battle together draws you together, no doubt—especially when it's for the life of your own child. What started out as a little cough that I thought Lundi picked up from one of our older kids was only the beginning of a test that would challenge us in ways we never imagined.

We were on summer vacation with my side of the family at a nearby lake house when I first noticed something was wrong with Lundi. She had become really lethargic, beyond the sleepy disposition of a newborn. In my gut, I knew something was off. With the slightest spike of a fever, Jason and I took off for the nearest emergency room.

The ER staff instantly started doing tests. Lundi and I were cuddled up on a bed under layers of sheets in the cold hospital room while Jason stood beside us, waiting to hear the results of her X-rays.

"Pneumonia," the doctor said.

"What?!?" I bolted upright in disbelief. I had taken Lundi to the doctor before we left for the lake and she had assured me the cough was nothing to be concerned about, especially since there was no fever at the time.

How did it escalate to pneumonia that fast? I questioned inwardly. It just didn't make sense. Little did I know that pneumonia would soon be the least of our worries.

About an hour later, a nurse came in to tell us they were transferring us to a children's hospital. Jason called my parents to let them know what was going on while I sat there sobbing, riddled with guilt as I looked down at Lundi, so innocent and helpless in my arms. *I am responsible for protecting and taking care of her. How did she develop pneumonia without me knowing?*

Once the ambulance dropped us off at the children's hospital, a female doctor met us in the hallway. She walked with us as medics placed Lundi into a small, mobile glass box with two round openings on each side.

The doctor's intensity and pace communicated the seriousness of it all. "Mom," she said to me in a soft but firm voice. "Fill me in—when did she first spike a fever? How long has she been coughing?"

Before I could answer, Lundi started to cough. Everyone stopped dead in their tracks. The doctor whipped out her stethoscope and stuck it through one of the openings of the box to listen to Lundi's chest.

It felt like my heart would break watching Lundi trying so desperately to gasp for air. Her coughs were getting more and more intense.

The doctor pulled her scope back and looked at us. "Okay, so here's the deal," she began. "I looked at her X-ray, and her right lung is not looking good. From the look of her X-rays and listening to her cough just now, I think she has pertussis."

"Pertussis?" I asked. "What's that?"

"It's also called whooping cough. For an adult, it's manageable. But for an infant, it presents many challenges. We won't get the official test results back for a couple days, so I'm going to keep her here with me and my staff. But I want to prepare you. If it is pertussis, then things are going to get worse—maybe much worse—before they get better."

She looked at me with empathetic eyes, as if we were fellow mothers talking. "Listen," she said, "your daughter's body is very small to fight pertussis, and there is little we can do in terms of medicine. It just has to run its course. All we can do is support her through it the very best we can." She reached out and touched my shoulder as she added, "And that's exactly what we are going to do."

I stood at attention, wide-eyed and nodding my head, taking mental notes as she continued to talk about what we might be dealing with. As soon as she left, I broke down in Jason's arms and sobbed. We held each other in that room, just the two of us and our little Lundi. In that moment, we both realized we were in for the fight of our lives. But it was a battle we were determined to win, and we would rely on God to bring the victory.

We laid hands on Lundi's tiny body and prayed for God to heal our little girl of this sickness. Afterward, I looked up *pertussis* on my phone to try to wrap my mind around what she was fighting.

"Often fatal in infants," one article read.

I couldn't go there. I put the phone back into my pocket. At this point, there were no more tears. There was no agonizing over *woulda, coulda, shoulda.* No room for guilt or fear or anything else. I felt a focus come over me that I can't explain.

My mindset became simple: *We have to win.*

But as the doctor had warned, things did get worse, and fast. Lundi coughed so much and so violently, we wondered how her little body could take it all. The next day, she was transferred to the intensive care unit. Her body swelled from all the medicine they pumped into her, and her face looked puffy. A large IV punctured the top of her tiny head while a tube went through her nose and throat. And there were all sorts of complications with her special feeding tube, leaving her voice box temporarily damaged. She would wake up crying frantically with no sound coming out.

All I could do was hold her little hand and sing "In the Name of Jesus" over and over until the song became a tired hum. It was an old hymn I sang while growing up that went, "In the name of Jesus, we have the victory. Who can tell what God can do? Who can tell of His love for you?" It ended with this phrase, "In the name of Jesus, Jesus, we have the victory."

I couldn't bear the thought of losing my baby, so I refused to think about it. I just kept my mind focused on those words. *Victory in Jesus. Victory in Jesus. We have the victory.* When I wasn't singing the words over Lundi, they played over and over inside my head, sustaining my heart.

Our church and mission-sending organization called a nationwide fast and prayer vigil for our little girl. We received messages from missionaries across the world telling us they were crying out for her life. One woman wrote and said she stayed up all night in Africa warring in prayer for Lundi.

What a humbling feeling that was, knowing God had raised up an army of warriors to fight alongside us in our moment of need. We felt our hearts knit with those who stood beside us during that time, doing battle on our behalf in the spirit. It gave us such a stunning and clear picture of the body of Christ. While an army of workers in the hospital did all they could to support Lundi physically, there was an army of believers supporting our family in prayer.

That's another aspect of battle we often take for granted, and one of the main reasons that getting involved in a local church is so important for a married couple. You weren't meant to fight alone. When you have others in your life who can help you in your time of need, it draws you close to those people. As a result, not only do you grow stronger as a couple, but the church grows stronger too. "And the gates of hell will not prevail against the church" (Matthew 16:18).

We've counseled many couples whose main problem was their lack of being in a community of like-minded believers. They were trying to fight on their own, and God didn't design people to thrive on their own. Husbands need other men. Wives need other women. Being a part of a church is a *must* if you're going to be victorious in the fight.

Lundi's body had to fight the sickness on its own, as the doctor had told us, but she was far from alone. As we called on the Great Healer to do His thing, I felt the power of those worldwide prayers in a supernatural way! I was focused and fixed on victory.

There was only a brief period when fear overcame me. It was during the most critical hours in the ICU and I hadn't slept in days.

"Just go lie down and sleep for a little bit," Jason said. "I'll stay right here with her."

"Promise you'll get me if anything changes?" I asked, arms resting on the bed rails opposite him, staring at our girl.

"I promise," he assured me. "Get some sleep."

Down the hall, I found a pitch-black room with a bed and no windows. I shut the door and lay down.

FLIGHT

Jason:

You may wonder why we're talking about our sick daughter in a book on marriage. But we have found that when you have a battle-ready mindset together with your spouse, the struggles that threaten to tear many couples apart will actually draw you together. This was one such struggle.

With Tori finally able to get away and rest, I sat next to Lundi's bed, watching her sleep peacefully. About an hour later, she jolted awake as she started coughing. I stood there, praying for her to stop, but she didn't. The more she coughed, the less she could breathe. The next thing I knew, her little body turned blue and alarms started going off on the machines that monitored her vital signs.

Instantly, a team of nurses rushed in. One of them pushed me aside and started pounding on Lundi's chest with a rubber mallet. I could hear her saying, "Come on, baby girl! Come on! Breathe!" She just kept coughing and coughing, never taking a breath, until her coughs got so faint and her vitals so low, I was afraid she was going to die right then and there.

My heart stopped. I knew I had to get Tori. With the nurses surrounding Lundi, I sprinted out of the room to find her .

I flung the door open. "Tori! Get up. Lundi stopped breathing!"

AND FIGHT

Tori:

I was startled awake when I heard the door bust open.

"What!?" I cried as I jumped out of bed and darted into the hallway.

"She stopped breathing," Jason said, out of breath from running down the hall. "The nurses are all in there working on her."

Tears streamed down my face as we ran down the hallway. By the time we got to the room, Lundi had stopped coughing and the nurses had the situation under control, but it didn't stop the pain I felt in my heart.

I walked over to her bed and grabbed her hand. "We can't lose her, Babe," I said to Jason as we both sat there crying. "I just… I just can't."

A few minutes later, one of the doctors walked into the room.

"I need to talk to you guys for a second," he said solemnly. "I just need to prepare you for the possibility of life support. If what just happened happens again, we are going to have to put Lundi into an induced coma and place her on a ventilator."

My heart beat out of my chest as I processed what he was telling us. The idea that my child might be put to sleep and have a tube pushed down her throat to breathe for her engulfed me in fear.

I wiped the tears from my face and walked over to Lundi's bedside. I picked up her tiny little hand, all black and blue from being poked and prodded. Her eyes were closed but her fingers latched on tightly to mine. I could see she was fighting.

And that was all I needed to bust through the fear that had such a tight grip on me.

I won't give in to the fear of losing her. If she's going to fight, then I'm going to fight, I told myself. I leaned down next to her head and sang, "Victory in Jesus, victory in Jesus, we have the victory." With every word, I felt more emboldened to trust God to heal our baby girl.

Jason stood right beside me, laying hands on Lundi as he cried out for God to spare her life. He prayed specifically that God would raise her up to be a modern-day Deborah in our culture.

That was *our* baby. Together, we were Heaven-bent to win this fight.

We spent many quiet nights together in that hospital room. Often with Bibles open, faces down, and few words between us, Jason and I were united. Fighting this fight together drew us together.

As Lundi held onto our fingers, we held onto God and each other, claiming the hope of victory in Jesus's name.

The next day, Lundi's cough got a little better, and the following day it was even better. As swarms of friends and family continued to pray, Lundi made it through the peak of her sickness without being placed on life support. Slowly but surely, she made a full recovery.

Two weeks after we took her to the hospital, she was released. The victory was *ours!* It was truly a victory in Jesus.

Today, our Lundi Mae is eleven years old—the picture of health, full of life and energy, and a constant reminder that we serve a God who heals. She has experienced *none* of the side effects the doctors assured us she would suffer.

I often think about this experience with Lundi when I went against my natural inclination toward fear and kept my eyes fixed on victory. I've realized the difference was my mindset. At first, the *coulda, woulda, shouldas* overwhelmed me. But the moment I learned what we were really dealing with, something shifted. My mind was set on victory. Because, quite honestly, my heart and mind could not operate under the weight of any other outcome.

I began to understand the importance of having a *victory mindset* and its power to transform my life and relationships. When we understand the seriousness of a situation, a victory mindset is *resolved* to win. This mindset acts as a secret weapon against the enemy.

Sometimes we don't know the real threat we're facing. Jason and I were freaking out over a case of pneumonia for our daughter when the truth was that she actually had pertussis. The minute we recognized the reality of this deadly sickness, our focus changed and a determination to win took over.

The power of having the right mindset is also true with marriage. If we recognize the real battle is for the life or death of our relationship, we can choose to put on a mindset of victory—one that says, "We *will* win!" This mindset rises above anything that would get in the way of victory.

This was how we were able to rekindle our old flame after Jason's crazy dream. We were intent on winning the battle for our marriage!

How you see the battle determines how you fight it. When there is a resolve for victory, something supernatural rises up inside you to do what is necessary to achieve it. But it doesn't always come naturally.

Sometimes the battle will be a physical trial, as with Lundi's sickness. Sometimes the fight will be spiritual—like the one Jason fought for me in prayer those many mornings. Sometimes the fight will be emotional—like the fight I had of overcoming fear and trusting God for another child. But having a winning mindset changes the way we fight.

These experiences showed me that God can breathe life into anything—a stale relationship, the heart of a tired mother, or the lungs of a sweet baby in the ICU. There is truly nothing our God can't do.

I still sing that old hymn the way I did in Lundi's hospital room. *Victory in Jesus. Victory in Jesus. We have the victory.*

A few short years after Lundi's birth, our family would be fighting for victory once again—not in a hospital, but on reality television.

KEY TAKEAWAY:

A mindset for victory is a must in your marriage. When life hits and you find yourselves in a very real struggle, fighting to win will pull you through. Things may not work out the way you want with the situation, but you will certainly have a stronger marriage than you did before the struggle.

QUESTIONS FOR CLOSER CONNECTION:

1. What's the biggest battle we're facing in our marriage right now?
2. Are our minds set on victory? Do we act like we can and will win, or are we living defeated?
3. What are some ways we can start operating by a victory mindset?

CHAPTER 18

THE BREAKUP

*"Sometimes, just believing in someone is enough for them
to start believing in themselves."*
– Kim Meeder

Jason:

"Guys, we're canceling the show."

Those were the words the top executive at HGTV said five weeks into a ten-week shoot in 2014. We were set to air a reality show on the real estate business my brother and I own. Maybe you've heard the story before. We tell all about it in our book *Whatever the Cost.*

Her statement was the culmination of a long battle between political activists and the network. The activists pressured HGTV to fire us because my brother and I had been outspoken about the biblical definition of marriage and about life beginning at conception.

According to these folks, we didn't deserve to have a reality show about our lives and business, much less to be on HGTV. They pulled out all the stops to make sure our show didn't see the light of day.

Their plan worked masterfully.

The crazy part is how cowardly my brother and I had been leading up to this conversation. We'd had a hunch it was coming. A week before the call, HGTV told us what was going on and that they would fight for us. "You guys are going to be stars on this network," our executive producer assured us.

But they weren't ready for the onslaught headed their way. When HGTV announced they were sticking with our show, one of the groups crafted a story that vilified us and our families and spread it all over social media. It made us look so bad that if even half of it were true, I would hate myself.

We didn't want to lose the platform the network had promised us, so the temptation to scrub the internet of anything we'd ever said regarding our pro-life and pro-marriage stand was very real. (Being totally honest here—we actually took down one video where we talked about the sanctity of human life and God's definition of marriage in the same clip. We've since put it back up, and it serves as a constant reminder to us of how cowardly we can be on our own.)

HGTV fought hard on our behalf, but in the end, they caved to the pressure. In the process, they lost millions, and *Flip It Forward* never aired an episode.

With that, David and I were left with a new narrative on the Benham brothers we never thought we'd have. We went from being known as successful Christian entrepreneurs who provided jobs for people and were an asset to society to being seen as hateful, bigoted, everything-phobic Bible thumpers who need imprisonment and/or death. No joke—people actually said they wished we were dead.

Fortunately, God knows our propensity for fear, so He put people around us to encourage us in the fight. My main encourager—the one by my side every step of the way—was Tori.

The word *encourage* actually means *to give someone courage*. To provide hope, support, and confidence. And if there's one thing you're supposed to do for your spouse, it's to help them feel and act courageously when they face a trial of their faith. When you do, the result is always a deeper emotional and relational connection.

This is what Tori did for me during one of the lowest points in my life.

A few minutes after our call with HGTV, a new reality began to set in—the type you can't catch on camera. I took a walk outside, my mind swirling.

I just got dumped, I thought as I paced back and forth. I didn't like the way it felt. It brought me right back to that seventh-grade birthday party where I was sidelined for someone more popular. Even though I had my head screwed on straight, the emotions were just as real as they had been when I was thirteen years old and Tiffany chose Ryan over me ... and as they were when I was twenty-five and the Baltimore Orioles released me. (More on this in the next chapter.)

A few hours after the call, as David and I were sitting in our office processing what had just happened, a buddy of ours who runs a marketing company walked in. "Hey guys," he said as he waved a piece of paper in his hand, "there are a bunch of local news stations that want to talk with you."

"Do what?" David asked.

"How did they find out what happened?" I added.

"I told them," he said. "When I heard what happened to you guys, I thought the story should be told."

"Well, that's just wonderful," I said, cringing at the idea. "I can't wait to go on TV to tell everyone why I just got dumped!"

But as we sat there with our heads spinning, we began to feel a real sense that we should do it. Neither of us wanted to, but we felt like God was calling us to it. After all, this wasn't a matter of being overlooked or left behind. This was a fight for our faith.

"Okay, we'll do it," we agreed.

After our friend left, David and I got down on our knees and asked God for strength.

Just before we said, "Amen," our buddy came back in. Actually, he ran in.

"Guys," he said as he tried to catch his breath, "there are so many stations that want the story I'm going to set up a press conference in the foyer of your office. They will all be here in an hour."

Oh, snap. This was going from nauseating to terrifying in a hurry! The butterflies in my stomach felt bigger than when I did cannonballs off the high dive at the Bradfield Park pool where David and I grew up. Neither of us wanted this type of drama in our lives, but we had said yes and couldn't back down now. It was time to suit up.

We jumped in our trucks to go home and change. News trucks were already starting to pull into our parking lot as we were leaving.

When I walked into the house, Tori smiled, gave me a big hug, and asked how I was feeling. "I'm okay," I said. "But I've got to hurry. I think almost every news station in Charlotte wants to talk to us."

The look on her face went from smiling and sentimental to concerned and confused.

"Are you serious?" she asked, her eyes wide in surprise. "What are you going to do?"

"We're going to talk to them, I guess," I said. "But I have no clue what to say."

The look on her face told me that she was nervous for me. But by the time I had changed clothes, so had her demeanor.

"God is doing something here." She put her hand in mine and I felt her quiet confidence. "Let me pray for you.

"God, please give Jason strength," she prayed. "Give him the words to speak. We pray that You would be glorified through this situation. And let him know I'm in this with him no matter what."

Even though my heart was pounding out of my chest, it felt

good to know I was not alone. I was comforted by the fact that whatever happened, my bride was right there by my side.

I rushed back out to my truck, drove to David's house to pick him up, and headed toward our office.

By the time we showed up, our parking lot was filled with news trucks. Our hearts were racing. We pulled in and just sat there. Neither of us wanted to go into the building.

We knew from experience the best thing you can do in moments like that is to hit them head-on and run toward the very thing you fear the most. We'd had a few occasions leading up to this where we had done quite the opposite. So, this time, we claimed Christ's promise: "Whenever you are arrested and brought to trial, do not worry beforehand about what to say. Just say whatever is given you at the time, for it is not you speaking, but the Holy Spirit" (Mark 13:11).

The minute we walked into the building, the busy crowd of reporters grew quiet. They all stared at us as lights beamed down on the desk-turned-podium where we stood to speak. Cameramen adjusted their lenses. Our marketing buddy gave us a thumbs-up, and off we went.

"If our faith cost us a reality show, then so be it ..."

Courage isn't the absence of fear. It's doing what's right in spite of it. We were scared senseless in that moment, but we could feel the Holy Spirit strengthening us to stand in faith and not cower in fear. And David and I knew we each had a faithful wife standing in our corner.

The conference went on for about twenty minutes. We said our part and then took questions. The main one was, "Why don't you just be quiet about your faith so you can keep your show?"

We explained that in today's culture, people don't mind you talking about God. Lots of television and movie stars do that. They just don't want you talking about the *boundaries* of God. But we believe God's blessings come within God's boundaries, and if those boundaries are removed, then blessings are replaced with burdens. If we really want to see people blessed, then we need to talk about the boundaries that bring those blessings.

Nobody argued with our line of thinking or our desire to stand for biblical values. At least, that day they didn't.

We left the building an hour later, relieved it was over and that we could move on with our lives. But just about that time, our buddy came running up to us again.

"I just got off the phone with CNN," he said, "and one of their main shows wants you on prime time tonight!"

"Oh, come on!" I thought we had just gotten through all this. "Are you serious?"

"Yeah, I'm serious," he said. "And they want you on another one in the morning. I think FOX News wants to talk to you too."

I think at this point David sprinted to the bathroom. Or it might have been me. The details are a little foggy.

Before we drove off, David looked over at me and said, "Well, I guess we have ourselves a new assignment."

All this took place at the same time the public debate was raging about legalizing same-sex marriage. Our view of upholding God's definition of marriage flew in the face of a politically correct and emotionally charged culture. Not only had we just been dumped by HGTV, but we found ourselves caught in the middle of this cultural firestorm—on the same day!

I dropped David off and headed home. All I thought was, *I just want to drive to the beach with Tori and the kids, away from the news and media and cameras and all that stuff.* I didn't like the idea of being "the reality stars who got fired for their faith."

At the same time, I felt a burning sense in my heart that we were doing the right thing and that God wanted us to walk this path. As much as I hated to admit it, David was right—this was our new assignment. We had no choice but to do it.

When I walked through the door, Tori wrapped her arms around my neck. "I'm so proud of you," she said as she held me tight. "I don't care what's being said—the kids and I know who you are and what is true. And we couldn't love you more."

Little did Tori know she was filling up a rapidly depleting love tank. When words of affirmation are your love language, hateful words aimed at you sting pretty badly. At this point, the Benham name was all over social media. People were saying all sorts of crazy stuff about us like, "Those brothers can take their Bibles with them on their way to Hell." I guess that's the new face of tolerance, inclusion, and love.

The thing that hurt the worst was that the first picture painted publicly about *the Benhams* was based on a lie. We were months away from being known by the world as successful real estate guys with a reality show, and now that was nothing more than a pipe dream.

Although I may have been calm on the outside, I was hurting on the inside. My brother David and I had spent years of our lives building a good reputation and we had based our business on that name, only to have it dragged through the mud. The feeling was like nothing I had faced before. One of our clients even stopped doing business with us while a franchisee distanced himself because of the media firestorm. Even more hurtful, several ministry partners asked if they could quietly separate from us.

We were getting a chance to see Christ's own words come to life: "Blessed are you when people insult you, persecute you, and *falsely* say all kinds of evil against you because of Me" (Matthew 5:11). There's no worse feeling than people believing something about you that is 100% false.

That evening, I told Tori about our upcoming CNN interview. "They are going to try to take our heads off. They hate everything we stand for. And to be honest, I'm scared to death!"

"Jase," she said confidently, "everything in your life has prepared you for this time. I've watched all that you've been through over the years and the way you've stood up for what's right. I've heard you speak the truth in love before, and you'll do it now. This is scary, no doubt, but you were made for this moment. You've got this!"

When she said those words, I felt like William Wallace in

Braveheart as he rode his horse over the hill with the blue war paint on his face to confront the British and defend his land. Everything inside me as a man stood at attention. My wife had just walked me to the battle line and gave me permission to fight… and to win.

Something clicked in me at that moment. I felt myself becoming the very warrior she believed me to be. She saw something in me that I didn't see, and she called it out of me.

Over the next two months, my brother and I participated in almost two hundred one-on-one interviews. From CNN to FOX News to ABC, Megan Kelly to *The O'Reilly Factor* to *Good Morning America*—we appeared on all of them. And by God's grace, we never backed down from our faith.

Armed with my new assignment from God and Tori's belief in me as a warrior, I didn't go on those shows to defend myself; I went on to encourage believers just as my wife had encouraged me. We encouraged Christians to stand for their faith whatever the cost and to never back down from what they know to be true.

I was in the fight of my life. But I went into it armed for battle because I had a wife who handed me the weapon I needed. That weapon was a belief that I was made for the fight I was entering. She believed in me, spoke to the warrior inside me, and I became the man she told me I was.

She gave me courage.

That's the power of marriage! Although Tori wasn't in front of the cameras, she was right there with me, handing me ammunition for the fight. She was right there in the trench with me.

The greatest reward of all was not that I stood and refused to back down; it was that fighting shoulder to shoulder with my wife drew us together as a couple. The public never saw any of that, of course, but Tori stood by me and never left me, even when it meant the name she took as her own would be ruined forever. If I was going down, she was going down with me.

We were in a fight for sure. But that fight brought new life to our marriage. No amount of reality TV stardom can beat that.

KEY TAKEAWAY:

Believing in your spouse is one of the most powerful things you can do. When you breathe life into your spouse it pulls out the best of who they are. Not only does your relationship benefit, but so does a world who needs what only they can offer.

QUESTIONS FOR CLOSER CONNECTION.
ASK YOUR SPOUSE:

1. Has there ever been a time I said or did something that put courage in you to face something difficult? What was it?
2. What did that moment mean to you? How did it help you overcome or get through the situation?
3. What are some ways I can encourage you with issues you're facing right now?

CHAPTER 19

BATTLE *BUDDY*

*"It is not a lack of love, but a lack of friendship
that makes unhappy marriages."*
– Friedrich Nietzsche

Tori:

All too often, couples lose sight of the power of simply being friends and how strong it can make them as a couple. The old saying, "Best friends, best married," is true. We've seen it dozens of times with couples who've talked with us in our living room. The ones who get past their differences the quickest are the ones who have a genuine friendship—they're buddies who haven't lost sight of the importance of having fun with each other.

Jason likes to say, "There is no stronger bond than friendship within the context of war. Ask any combat veteran: When friendship and fighting are aimed at the proper enemy, the two are a match made in Heaven." (He likes all that "fight" lingo!)

That's why we place so much emphasis in counseling on the importance of being battle *buddies*. (And, for the record, Jason's Baptist roots gets the credit for the *battle buddy* alliteration.)

It's not enough to simply engage in the fight—you need to do it with your best friend.

Before Jason and I got married, we were always planning the next fun thing to do together. Whether it was going on hikes, skiing, two-stepping, or doing a workout together, these were the moments that drew us close, that turned us into best friends. No matter what it was, it was just more fun if Jason was with me.

I wasn't aware of it at the time but something about being *active* and *playful* with Jason made him open up to me in ways he otherwise wouldn't—maybe even couldn't. I wish I would have picked up on the reality that most of our best conversations while dating took place while doing something active together.

On that note, can I let you ladies in on something that would have been helpful to know much earlier on in our marriage? In general, men are better communicators when they are moving. Most of my best conversations with my sons are rebounding for them or pretty much any activity that involves a ball. My youngest son and I hit a tennis ball back and forth on the driveway with some rackets we found in the garage this week and I don't even think he picked up that I was asking questions. He just answered them.

Honestly, it's not always easy … but it can be that simple. The same unintentional ways you fell in love, if done intentionally, will keep there. And maintaining *BFF* status with your spouse will serve your relationship best. Talk to any older couple that has the type of relationship you want—you'll find out they are best friends.

Jason:

I remember the first time I recognized the power of fun and genuine friendship in our relationship, and just how much it bonded me closely to Tori.

I was in my third year of professional baseball with the

Baltimore Orioles, stationed in Frederick, Maryland, with the Class A Minor League team, the Frederick Keys. It was an extremely important year for me professionally. The year before, I had snapped my leg in half in a collision at first base, so the "powers that be" in the baseball world were watching me closely to see how I had recovered. Two months into the season, I could tell I had lost a step, and my sub-par batting average showed it.

I'll never forget the day I arrived at the ballpark early and, while walking toward the clubhouse, I noticed shoe marks in the dirt around second base. That was my position.

My heart sank. I knew what that meant. *The coach must have asked one of the guys to take fielding practice at my position,* I thought as I stared blankly at the ground. *I bet the Orioles are thinking about … oh no, I can't go there.* The anxiety hit me like a tsunami.

Fear is often about a past or present threat while anxiety is about a potential future threat—specifically the anticipated event of powerlessness. I wasn't aware of these concepts at the time, but when I saw the field that day, I felt powerless over my future in baseball.

I had a hard time controlling my spiraling emotions. I was determined not to let it affect me in front of the guys, but inside, my heart was screaming. I wanted to be *wanted.* When the Orioles drafted me, they wanted me. Now I felt like they couldn't wait to get the jersey off my back.

I went over to my good buddy, Joey Hammond, who played shortstop, and asked, "Did they work someone out at second today?"

He looked back at me with empathetic eyes as if to say, *I'm sorry, dude.* Whispering so our manager couldn't hear, he said, "They worked Lopez out a few hours ago."

Joey and I both knew what that meant.

I felt a burning sensation deep in my gut. It was the same thing I had felt the year before as I lay in a hospital bed with a compound fracture in my right leg and a plaster cast all the way up to my hip. I had thought my dream of baseball was over and I'd never play again.

I went into the bathroom and stepped into one of the stalls to get away from the other players. In that moment of brief solitude, I prayed. "God, I don't know if this is my last day as a pro baseball player or not, but I ask You for the strength to get through this."

In spite of feeling desperate, I also felt determined—desperate for God's help but determined to power through the game and not show any emotion.

I wasn't in the lineup that night, but I had the best seat in the house—right next to the other players who sat the bench. We ate sunflower seeds the whole game and told jokes. I did everything I could to mask my anxiety over what I felt was coming.

In the last inning, we were up to bat when our first-base coach yelled over to the manager. "Hey, Skip!" he said. Our manager, Mack, looked over at him. He then pointed at me and made a swinging motion with his arms.

I knew what that meant—Let's give Benham a chance to hit.

If you know anything about baseball, this isn't a good sign. He wanted to give me a token chance to hit in the last inning of a mop-up game as an act of charity.

At that moment, I felt like everything went into slow motion. I had become the kid at the playground picked last because nobody wanted him. I looked down at Mack, who just shook his head, dismissing the idea. The ache in my gut ripped into a full-fledged wound.

The game ended and all the guys headed to the clubhouse. I was determined to stay outside as long as I could. If this was my last game as an Oriole, I would make it last as long as possible. So, I walked over to the stands and signed autographs for every person there.

About twenty minutes later, as I was surrounded by dozens of fans, I heard our clubhouse manager yell out, "Benham, Mack wants to see you in his office!"

He'll just have to wait, I thought as I dug in my emotional heels, determined I would sign every last person's autograph. I think I was just trying to control what little I could.

Ten minutes later, as the final fan left the stadium, I walked into the clubhouse. My heart pounded faster with every step I took. There was a hushed silence in the room. What I didn't know at the time was that our left fielder had just gotten released. And in a baseball clubhouse, when someone gets released, the TV gets turned off and the music stops blaring. A quiet, somber mood takes over because all the guys know full well it could be their turn next.

Sure enough, it was my turn.

I knocked on the manager's door. "Hey, Mack. You wanted to see me?"

"Yeah, Tex." He waved me in. "Tex" was what all the coaches called me, since I was from Texas.

"Listen, there's no other way to say this," he said as he shifted in his chair, "but we've got to let you go."

My chest instantly grew hot. Even though I knew this was coming, nothing could prepare me to actually hear the words. I felt a lump forming in my throat and tried to fight it back, but as I sat in silence, my lip began to quiver and tears started rolling down my cheeks.

He continued, "I've had to release a lot of guys in my years as a manager, but this one is especially tough. Everyone knows how hard you've worked to get here, and everyone in the organization loves you. But we have to move on."

He then got up from his desk and hugged me.

There's nothing like giving it your all only to hear someone say you're not good enough. When I injured my leg, I knew this day might come, but it didn't soften the blow when it finally fell. I felt broken all over again.

I walked out of Mack's office and sat down at my locker with my head in my hands, tears hitting the floor. I tried to stop crying, but I couldn't. Thoughts of what baseball had meant to me for so many years flooded my mind—playing catch in the back yard with Dad, listening to Mom ring her cowbell, taking batting practice with David, hearing my grandpa scream, "Fire it in there!"

Each one of the guys walked over and gave me a hug. I appreciated the gesture, but it did little to heal the aching void inside.

By the time I showered, changed, and packed up my locker, everyone in the stadium had left. I went to a payphone and called the one person whose voice I wanted to hear more than anyone's—Tori.

The instant I heard her voice, I started to cry again. Playing professional baseball wasn't just my dream alone. Tori shared it with me and was looking forward to joining the journey as my wife.

"I just got released," I told her. I could hear her gasp on the other line. She wasn't expecting that.

"I'm so sorry, Babe," she said, her voice warm and full of concern.

We both cried.

It felt good to know she was in this fight with me. We talked for a while longer, but before we hung up, she said, "Hey, why don't you drive up here to spend some time with me? Let's just have fun together. I have a good idea."

Those were the best words I'd heard in a long time. The thought of forgetting baseball and just hanging out with her—eating ice cream and laughing and watching movies and dancing in her kitchen—made baseball seem small at that moment.

I got up early the next morning and drove the six hours to Torrington, Connecticut. Her mom made an epic dinner, as usual. After we finished eating, I asked Tori about this idea she'd had.

"I was thinking about taking you to Six Flags tomorrow," she said with a bright smile on her face. "We can ride roller coasters and watch shows and have a picnic and eat fried dough.

It will be so fun!" At this point she was bouncing up and down and clapping with excitement like our youngest daughter does now when she's trying to talk us into one of her grandiose ideas.

Then she wrapped her arms around my neck and said, "I want you to forget all this stuff and just have fun with me."

For a hurting man who'd just been fired, her energy and enthusiasm were contagious. I loved the idea and was even more excited about how fun she was as a person.

By the time we were ready to leave the next morning, Tori had already packed a lunch full of her best homemade Italian grinders. Her parents jumped in on the action and gave us money for the tickets. I think her dad felt bad that I was jobless.

That day is my fondest memory of our dating years. One day, I was taking batting practice in an Orioles jersey, heartsick at the idea of getting released. Two days later, I was riding the Superman roller coaster next to Tori without a care in the world.

Tori wasn't just helping me have fun that day; she was actively mending my heart.

BFF

Looking back at that day in the theme park, what sticks out most is how good our friendship was. We weren't just boyfriend and girlfriend; we were buddies. Best buddies.

In studying for my master's degree and throughout the years since, I've read dozens of books on relationships and listened to hundreds of lectures by people who are much smarter than I am about helping couples get along. Most agree that one of the best things you can do to ensure a lasting relationship is to build a solid friendship.

I remember the feeling I used to get when I was a bored kid at home in Garland, Texas, and I'd hear Chad Scott knock on the door and say, "Can Jason and David come out and play?" Those are the best words any young kid can hear.

Tori did this for me during the most difficult time in my

life, and it worked. She pulled me out of a depressed state that easily could have thrust me into a cave where I kept all my emotions. She pulled me out by luring me from my discouragement with an opportunity to play.

Dr. John Gottman believes the determining factor for marital satisfaction between a husband and wife is the quality of their friendship. The happiest marriages are based on a deep friendship. He said that "friendship fuels the flame of romance because it is the best protection against feeling adversarial toward your spouse."[29]

Tori helped me through my battle because she chose to be my buddy. That's what we mean when we talk about being *battle buddies* together. Yes, you need to recognize you're in a battle and that you were meant to fight together. But you also have to realize that the best way to fight the battle is by having a foundation of being friends—you and your spouse together as best buddies, doing the things that make you laugh.

Fighting together draws you together. But so does laughing together. Laughter relaxes the body, boosts the immune system, triggers the release of feel-good endorphins in the brain, protects your heart, burns calories, and can even help you live longer.[30] So if your spouse can help you laugh, they are actually helping you heal.

When Tori and I counsel couples struggling with perpetual conflict, one of the things we tell them about is the power of humor to extinguish the anger that results from butting heads. If they can figure out a way to make each other laugh in the midst of a fight, it will cool the negative tension that can otherwise keep them apart.

When Tori and I get into an argument, one of us will almost always say or do something that makes the other laugh. That's what buddies do. We still laugh about the stupid things we have said in the heat of arguments.

One time, just a few years into marriage, we got into an argument over money. Tori got so mad she wadded up a five-dollar bill and threw it at me and yelled, "Here! Wipe your butt with this!"

Wow. No words even came to my mind in response to a line like that. So, I took the bill, unfolded it, and made a wiping motion as if I were actually doing what she told me to do. We both busted out laughing so hard we forgot what we were even fighting about.

To this day, we use that line at times to break the tension. "Wipe your butt with this" is a hard line to say without laughing.

Fortunately for me, a few days after our theme-park adventure, I landed a job in Torrington as the hitting coach for the summer league team I had played for three years earlier. Tori and I would get to pal around all summer long.

Halfway through that summer, on a night when we didn't have a game, I got down on one knee in the church where we first met and asked Tori to be my best friend for life. I slid that ring on her finger, and we've been best buddies ever since.

KEY TAKEAWAY:

Don't ever lose sight of being best friends with your spouse. Add some fun into your marriage to strengthen your friendship. Do things together. The stronger your friendship the healthier your relationship.

QUESTIONS FOR CLOSER CONNECTION.
ASK YOUR SPOUSE:

1. What are some ways I was a good friend to you before we got married?
2. Am I a good friend to you now? How so?
3. How can I be a better friend?

CHAPTER 20

CROSSFIT *NOW*

*"Progress is impossible without change; and those who
cannot change their minds cannot change anything."*
– George Bernard Shaw

Tori:

Jason is good at CrossFit. He has the natural body composition, athleticism, and work ethic to be good at that style of workout, which makes him highly capable of winning team competitions. (I know, I already said all this near the beginning of the book, but I'm going somewhere with it.)

When we first started CrossFit, tasting victory on Saturdays together was a great motivation for us to come back for more. Fighting together drew us together, remember?

But that all changed for us a few years ago, causing us to redefine what victory at CrossFit looks like.

After an intense workout that involved box jumps, Jason's knee hurt pretty badly. It was the leg he had broken back when he was with the Orioles … and the same knee that suffered a torn ACL just after he retired from baseball.

He had been injury-free for several years at that point, so

when his knee started hurting again, he was scared. After a visit to the doctor, his worst fear was confirmed—he had torn his ACL again and would need surgery to fix it.

He swore the damage had happened a few weeks previously when he gave blood for a physical at his doctor's office and passed out while sitting in a chair, but I'm not sure I believe it. Those competitive juices running through his veins wouldn't let him scale back on the intense workouts he loves so much. Until he had no choice.

After surgery, the doctor told Jason to take it easy for a while. "Just listen to your body," he advised. "You'll know when you're ready and how much you can push yourself. If you go too hard, you'll find yourself in here a third time."

However, for someone who has pushed himself beyond his natural limits in sports his whole life, taking this advice wasn't as simple as it might sound. Apparently, when you "push through the pain" long enough, you can lose the instinct of knowing when to stop.

Soooo, about a year after his second ACL surgery, Jason found himself locked in an intense Saturday team workout, pushing himself like he was accustomed to doing. Then, in the middle of doing squats, the screw that held his ACL in place popped out of his knee. No joke. I can't make this stuff up. He had to get two guys to carry him to the car.

As I drove him home that morning with his leg propped up on the dashboard and a pin sticking out like a peg underneath his skin, I begged him to stop pushing his body beyond its limits. The problem was that his mindset about workouts had become so ingrained after years of practice that he had no idea how to shut it off. A few weeks later, we were back in the hospital to repair the leg.

I can honestly say, this time it worked—he finally came to a place where he changed his mindset about CrossFit. "I'm done with this," he slurred as the nurse pushed his wheelchair to the car from the surgery center. "I'm never coming back to this place again." He was sleepy with one eye closed. He looked a lot like he did the other two times, and I wasn't so sure about his drug-induced proclamation.

Something changed in Jason after that third surgery, though. He began to see that there are other ways to win at the gym. Victory in his workouts started to look less like beating the other guys and more like simply walking out of the gym without limping. And because I'm not at all interested in nursing a fourth surgery, I've become pretty good at giving him *that* look—the one that says, *Put the bar down and back away slowly with your hands up!*

Jason and I don't win team workouts anymore. In fact, we don't attend on Saturdays as much as we used to. Team competitions have been replaced with bodyweight boot camps—a class with no winners or losers.

The "win" for us has changed. We still love working out together, but it doesn't look like it used to. As hard as it was for Jason to make this change, we find ourselves enjoying this new season of life where fiercely competitive workouts have been replaced with simply elevating our heart rates. But if our mindsets were stuck on how we *used* to win workouts, we would probably lose the motivation to show up at all.

Maintaining a winning mindset in battle is crucial in marriage. But as we grow in our relationships, we discover that winning doesn't always look the same. Things change as we grow and mature—and that's okay!

Through our ten years at CrossFit, we've learned there are different victories for different seasons. Our goal now is to simply stay healthy and energetic, and to be in community with others who share our passion for health and fitness. While the win looks different, it still feels like a win nonetheless.

Truth is, there would be little motivation to show up had we not redefined what victory looks like to us now. Jason would have just kept getting hurt and, ultimately, we'd have quit going.

Maybe you have reached a place like this in your marriage.

Perhaps it's time to redefine what victory looks like for you and your spouse. Time to stop comparing it to what it used to be or how you see it in others.

Maybe you have simply lived your way into a new season and victory doesn't look like it used to. Without the hope of the type of victory you've always had in mind, perhaps you have lost the motivation to show up. If that's the case, the answer is simple—redefine it!

We've seen too many couples struggle with changing their mindset when it comes to embracing a new stage in life. As a result, they find themselves unable to truly connect with each other because they're living in the past or stuck in a never-ending cycle of comparison. It's a hopeless, demotivating place to be.

Before Jason and I got married, we loved going to a full day at an amusement park or finding a place to go country dancing. Today, we get motion sick if we even see a roller coaster, and most of our dancing takes place across the hardwood in our house. We used to hit the town on our Friday night date night like clockwork, but it's turned into takeout and a romantic comedy in our room because "playdates" for our oldest kids have turned co-ed around here.

But we are still winning. It's important that we keep this mindset.

"Different" doesn't translate as a loss. The win is that we are still doing things that draw us close. Like crushing good food together, even if it's in our bedroom. We know this season won't last forever and we'll be right back to hitting up our old familiar Friday night spots.

The win in your marriage may look like it used to or maybe it's changed with the times. Either way, victory in marriage is all about the mindset. It's the ability to see the win in all situations and go after it.

Your mindset about your marriage involves doing one of two things: winning or losing. I can assure you, a winning mindset results in a winning marriage.

But it's up to you to define—or redefine—what it looks like.

FAMILY TIES

A picture hangs in my parents' dining room where our entire family gathers every week for Sunday lunch. It has a quote by Walt Whitman that says, "We were together, I forget the rest."

This has become the victory for my parents.

Sunday lunches with our whole family started many years ago. One grandchild has turned into eight. Orderly calm has turned to organized chaos. But one thing remains: we are together. That's the victory for my mom and dad. That mindset has given them the stamina and the energy week after week, year after year, to bring all of us together over and over and over again.

They fight for that time because they have defined what victory looks like for their family—it's all of us being together, regardless of how crazy it is. And they take it all in. They are so thankful for family time that they are actually energized by a house full of crazy kids and a sink full of pots and pans. (At least, they act like they are!)

Mom and Dad's ability to define victory has blessed our family beyond measure. Their minds are set and it has brought us all together as a family—because that's what we are. Like CrossFit for me and Jason, the victory has to be redefined at times. Just a few weeks ago, only six of the twenty family members were able to make lunch—all of whom had the last name Benham.

"I wish you guys wouldn't have done all this for just us," I told my parents as Jason and the kids happily filled their plates to sit around the big table with many empty chairs.

"God knew we needed some intimate time with just you guys," Mom said as Dad winked at me in agreement. "This is perfect."

That Sunday meal around my parents' table was a win because my parents had the ability at a moment's notice to redefine it. A win for that day wasn't a table for twenty but a table for eight.

Once you can see the victory in your current battle, whatever it might be, you'll move toward it. You'll discover the beauty in battle because you're in a fight you can win. (And hopefully you won't need to tear your ACL to see how pretty that victory can be!)

The fact is, we were designed with a desire to win. We are reward-driven people for a purpose. Winning is motivating and energizing. It gets us moving in the direction God has for us.

If we hadn't redefined victory at CrossFit, we wouldn't be showing up at all on Saturdays. The same is true in marriage: if you can see the win—whatever it may be in that moment—you will keep showing up.

KEY TAKEAWAY:

Your mindset about your marriage involves doing one of two things: winning or losing. A winning mindset results in a winning marriage. But it's up to you to define—or redefine—what it looks like. As you grow and mature in marriage winning might not look like what it used to, but that's ok. So long as you are in it together, you'll have the energy to stay in the game.

QUESTIONS FOR CLOSER CONNECTION.
ASK YOUR SPOUSE:

1. What was your idea of "winning" in marriage when we started out?
2. Has anything happened to change that?
3. In our current stage of life, what does our win look like now?

CHAPTER 21

GO GET 'EM!

*"Don't pick a fight, but if you find yourself in one,
I suggest you make darn sure you win."*
– John Wayne

Everything changed for us when we realized we were made for a fight. We discovered the beauty of marriage when we entered the battle for our relationship. When we chose to stop fighting against each other in personal battles but alongside one another in a spiritual war, we saw firsthand how fighting together drew us together. The conflict that once separated us now strengthened us. Over our twenty-plus years together, we have become *battle buddies* and now experience the power of a relationship built on a battle-ready mindset.

We desperately want this for you in your marriage.

God created us for a spiritual fight. This fight will continue until His foe is ultimately vanquished and all believers share a meal together on the threshold of eternity: The Wedding Feast of the Lamb, discussed in Revelation chapter 19. It will be the greatest family gathering you've ever experienced, when Christ will finally embrace His Bride—the Church—and usher us into His presence forever.

The wedding that opened the Bible is nothing like the

wedding that closes it. Our earthly marriages are simply a shadow of this spiritual marriage.

Until that time, God has equipped us for the battle at hand by giving us a spouse with whom we can stand boldly against our enemy. But until we recognize this spiritual call to arms, we will never experience the full depth of relational intimacy for which He has created us.

Ever since the very first relationship was formed, our adversary has sought to break down and break up this vital connection between husband and wife. He comes at our most vulnerable moments to make accusations for our agreement. He wants to keep us defeated in our own personal battle over sin and occupied in a relational battle against each other, resulting in us being nothing more than powerless pawns in the Kingdom battle for the hearts and souls of people. He accomplishes this by distracting us with temptation, deceiving us with lies, and dividing us from those we love.

But God has given us the strength and power to overcome. We can be victorious in our personal battle against sin, free from relational battles against each other, and powerful in the Kingdom battle for our families. We accomplish this by refusing to agree with the accuser—by recognizing the enemy's attack, renouncing the lie behind the temptation, and replacing it with the truth.

This is how we walk in victory as a couple and transform into a battle-tested war machine that defeats darkness and draws close to each other in the process. As we focus on God and move closer to Him individually, we draw closer to each other relationally.

But this isn't the full story. There's a foundation for the fight that gives us the solid footing we need to duke it out on the battlefield. It comes in the words of God the Father to His Son, Jesus, just before He entered His own battle against the enemy.

We talked earlier about how Jesus entered a personal battle against Satan in the wilderness—how He walked into the fight "full" of the Spirit and He walked out in the "power" of the Spirit. He went from "full" to "powerful" by refusing to agree with the accuser and give in to the temptations that came His way.

But we rarely think about what happened just before, how God the Father prepared His Son for the fight.

The story starts with a man named John the Baptist, who had been preaching and proclaiming the good news that the long-awaited Messiah, the Savior of Israel, was alive and would soon make Himself known. Anticipation mounted as the crowds swelled, hanging onto John's every word. Everyone was looking for a king who would deliver them from Roman oppression and fulfill the prophecies spoken centuries before.

Jesus *was* that king. But He didn't come to reign as a *physical* king on the throne in Jerusalem—He came as a *spiritual* king to sit on the throne of the human heart. However, His kingdom would not come without a fight. Satan would do everything in his power to get Jesus to sin so he could keep his title as prince of the earth.

Jesus showed up one day and asked John to baptize Him. John granted His request and baptized the Savior of the world.

Just as Jesus came up out of the water, Heaven was opened and the Spirit of God descended on Him. Then God spoke audibly to His Son.

Let's stop here for a moment.

Before we share what God said, we need to remember what He knew at that very moment: His boy was about to enter the fight of His life. Satan was prepared to pounce.

What would the Father say to prepare the Son for this battle of the ages?

As Jesus came up out of the water, God said, "This is my Son, whom I love; with Him I am well pleased" (Matthew 3:17).

God said three things very clearly to His Son:

You're mine: "This is My Son …"

I love you: "Whom I love …"

I like you: "With Him I am well pleased."

These three statements armed Jesus for the battle and became the foundation from which He could withstand the attacks of the enemy. And I'm sure when the going got tough in the wilderness, it was these words from His Father that Christ remembered. They energized Him for the fight.

"Then Jesus was led up by the Spirit into the wilderness to be tempted by the devil" (Matthew 4:1). Armed with His Father's encouragement, Christ entered the fiercest battle in history against Satan himself and emerged the champion.

One of the greatest things you can do for your spouse is to equip them for the fight by communicating the same thing to them that God did to Jesus:

"You're mine."

"I love you."

"I like you."

Say it with your words and live it with your actions.

Husbands, your wife will know she's yours when you come home from work and put your phone away, making her the priority. She'll feel your love for her when you help clean up after dinner and play with the kids in the yard. She'll know that you like her when you snuggle in bed and watch a chick flick rather than a game with the guys.

Wives, your husband will know he's yours when you surprise him with his favorite meal. He'll feel your love when you affirm him in his work and admire his work ethic. He'll know you like him when you snuggle up on the couch to watch a game rather than a chick flick alone in your room.

But here's the real beauty—this isn't just something you say to your spouse and your spouse says to you. It's something God wants to say to you. He wants you to know that you are His, that He loves you, and He likes you.

Pause for a minute and think about that. Say each of those things to yourself right now and know that God feels them for you. "You're mine. I love you. I like you." He wants to pour His love on you right now, right where you are, whether you're reading this book or listening to it on audio. These are His thoughts toward you. Receive them. Believe them. They are for you.

Do you know one of the best ways God communicates His love to you? Through your spouse!

Wives, when your husband comes home early from work to be with you, that's God saying *through him* that you're His. When he helps out around the house and plays with the kids, that's God saying He loves you. When he puts his arm around you and pulls you close, that's God reminding you that He likes you.

Husbands, when your wife surprises you with your favorite meal, that's God saying *through her* that you're His. When she affirms you in your work and admires your work ethic, that's God saying He loves you. When she snuggles up under your arm to watch the game, that's God reminding you that He likes you.

Not only is your spouse God's gift to you, but you are God's gift to your spouse. Don't forget that. You are the conduit through which God makes His love known to His son or daughter. God is not just your Father, remember—He's your Father-in-Law.

Your marriage is not ultimately about you and your spouse. It's about you and Jesus. Marriage is simply the opportunity to live and love like Him. It's God's way of showing you how much He loves you and likes you.

This is the foundation for the fight.

Jesus would need this encouragement from the Father, as He would soon be fulfilling the greatest battle of all—one in which He would be "pierced through for our transgressions … crushed for our iniquities; the punishment that brought us peace was on Him, and by his *stripes* we are healed" (Isaiah 53:4 BSB, emphasis added).

The Hebrew word for "stripe" is *habbura*, which means "blows." It comes from the root word *habar*, which means "to be joined, coupled, heaped up … to *bind*."[31] The suffering Christ endured *binds* us to Him. But only if we're willing to suffer for Him as He suffered for us (Romans 8:17).

Those who suffer together stay together.

Those who fight together draw together.

Jesus fought the greatest battle of all and came out the victor. He promises the same for us as we are faithful in the battles that come our way. The result will be a binding with Him that cannot be broken. And when we fight these battles alongside our spouse, they draw us closer to each other just as they do in our relationship with Christ.

God wants to use you to equip your spouse for the fight, just as He did for His Son. The question is, will you let Him?

There's beauty in battle. We win in marriage when we wage a war—not against each other as enemies but alongside one another as allies against the enemy of our marriage. God put us in a fight and equipped us for the battle by giving us the greatest gift of all—a battle buddy who completes us in every way. It's time for you and your spouse to step into this fight. When you do, you'll discover how fighting together draws you together.

There will be times you feel weary of the fight or reluctant to don your spiritual armor to wage yet another battle. But during those times, look over and let your hope be rekindled by your spouse fighting by your side. Look up, knowing your Savior has accomplished the greatest battle on your behalf. And embrace the eternal hope that one day we'll be able to put down these weapons once and for all, sit side by side, and enjoy a heavenly wedding like none other.

Remember, the Bible opens and closes with a wedding. Marriage is a part of God's answer to the problem of evil in the world. Your marriage was made for the fight. You were created for battle. It's time for you to win in marriage by waging a war.

FORGIVENESS REDEFINED

*"To forgive is to set a prisoner free and discover
that the prisoner was you."*
– Lewis B. Smedes

Tori:

There's not a single marriage in existence where forgiveness isn't necessary. While there's beauty in the midst of battle, oftentimes it doesn't happen apart from a few mishaps along the way. The nature of warfare is that people make mistakes, and when the inevitable happens, forgiveness is the only thing that keeps you together.

Over the years, we've seen unforgiveness as one of the main issues that keep couples from experiencing the power that God wants them to have in their relationship.

At the same time, blindly forgiving someone who hasn't repented can be equally as destructive.

We counseled one such couple a few years ago.

Blake and Jessica came to see us two years into their marriage. While they truly loved each other, they just couldn't find a way to manage the increasing conflict they were experiencing.

The first time they came to see us, Jessica started crying as she described their situation. When Blake reached over to grab Jessica's hand, she jerked it back and gave him the look of death. Since anger is often a mask for pain, I knew we needed to dig a little deeper to get to the root. So, I cautiously began to ask a few more questions, specifically about her past.

In time, I could see that Jessica was struggling with one of the main things that keeps people locked in a perpetual cycle of defeat in the personal battle and consistently occupied in the relational battle—unforgiveness. She needed to experience the power of forgiveness in her life by choosing to forgive those who had hurt her so long ago.

I knew this was Jason's wheelhouse. He has had to walk through several situations in business where people cheated him. In the process, he discovered a new way of seeing forgiveness that set him free from the anger that often accompanies the pain.

Jason:

The minute I saw that Jessica had a forgiveness issue, I couldn't help but jump in. I had been freed from that burden just a few years earlier, so I shared what I had learned through my own experience.

"When you refuse to forgive someone, you give them power over you," I told her. "When you forgive, not on the basis of the person deserving it but on the basis of God's forgiveness toward you, you are the one who is set free."

I could see the wheels turning in her head. My guess was that whoever hurt her in the past had never apologized for it and made it right.

"We're told in the Bible to forgive as God forgives," I said. "Do you think God forgives an unrepentant person?" I asked.

"No," she responded.

"That's right," I said. "God forgives those who repent, those who ask for forgiveness. If we blindly forgive someone who hasn't repented, then we trample God's justice. God's justice is meant to lead people to Him. They need to first feel condemnation for what they've done. Then, when they repent, God can forgive them. Their repentance restores their relationship with God."

"So, what do we do when someone wrongs us but doesn't repent?" she asked.

"Well, we can't hold unforgiveness in our heart," I said. "Otherwise, we'd be sinning. Rather, we do what Jesus did when He was on the cross. He said, 'Father, forgive them.'"

She and Blake both looked a little puzzled. It's the way Tori and I felt the first time we tried to wrap our minds around this concept of forgiveness.

"We know Jesus had the power to forgive sins," I continued, "because He said to the paralyzed man in Mark 2:5, 'Your sins are forgiven.' When Jesus forgave him, He saw the man's heart and could tell he was truly repentant. So, He granted forgiveness. But on the cross, He knew those who took part in putting Him there were unrepentant. He wanted them to experience forgiveness, but they first had to be brought to repentance, so He asked God to handle the situation."

I could tell she was thinking deeply, so I pushed the idea a little further.

"Jesus had forgiveness in His heart and would freely give it to those who repented," I explained. "But until they repented, He gave the situation to God and let Him handle it. In the meantime, He was free."

"That kind of makes sense," she said. "I've always had a hard time with the thought of forgiving someone who isn't sorry."

"Choosing to forgive someone who's unrepentant is not following Christ's example of forgiveness," I said. "But we can't walk around with unforgiveness in our hearts. Choosing to forgive is doing the same thing Christ did on the cross when He gave the situation to God. It now becomes a transaction between you and God—the other person is no longer your problem and has no power over you."

The couple nodded in understanding.

"From this point forward," I continued, "when the people who hurt you come to mind, ask God to bring them to repentance so they can experience the same forgiveness you have received. This will keep you from growing bitter toward them. Then, if they repent to you, grant them forgiveness. If they don't, trust God to bring them to that point. Either way, you are free!"

"Okay," she said with a look that said, *I'll give it a shot.*

The next time we saw them, Jessica was a different person, and their relationship was finally on the right track.

"I feel so free," she said. "I wish I would have known this earlier."

"Your only responsibility," I said, "is to teach others the same."

I then explained to her an easy way to keep it straight in your mind. It goes like this:

When someone wrongs you and repents, do what Jesus did with the paralyzed man—grant forgiveness. No matter how bad their sin against you was, your responsibility in light of Christ's great sacrifice is to grant them the same forgiveness God gave to you.

But when someone wrongs you and they don't repent, do what Jesus did on the cross—give the situation to God and let Him handle it. In the meantime, you stay "ready to forgive." This will keep you from walking around in unforgiveness, which will only harm you and those you love. In the process, you trust God to handle the situation.

Maybe this is something you're struggling with right now. If so, contemplate which scenario fits your situation and work through it with God. Maybe the person has repented and you need to grant forgiveness. Do it as Jesus did with the paralyzed man, understanding that the emotional scars will take time to heal. During that time, erect some boundaries to protect yourself and the relationship. These boundaries act like a cast on a broken bone, assuring that healing can take place.

If the person hasn't repented, do what Jesus did on the cross and give the situation to God. Do not blindly forgive. If you do so, then your sense of justice will be trampled on and it won't sit right. Deep down, you'll know justice needs to be served. When you give the situation to God, you are releasing the issue and no longer holding onto unforgiveness. In this way, you will be free.

"So if the Son sets you free, you are free indeed" (John 8:36).

IN THE BEGINNING

"In the beginning God created the heavens and
the earth ...and marriage."
– paraphrase of Genesis 1

Have you ever noticed how the Bible opens with a marriage and closes with one? In Genesis 2, it opens with the marriage of Adam and Eve. In Revelation 22, it closes with the marriage between Christ and the church.

Having written several books, I can tell you that the most important part of any book is how you open it and how you close it. So, when God chooses marriage as the bookends to Scripture, we ought to pay close attention to the value of that relationship and the role it plays in the extension of His kingdom.

Sandwiched between these two nuptial agreements is the story of a battle – a spiritual fight between the forces of good and the forces of evil. Marriage, as we saw in chapter five, is the warring mechanism God created to fight this battle. And the more connected we stay to each other, the stronger we are to defeat the devil and prepare him for his ultimate doom.

This is why fighting together draws us together. God created us this way. The nature of war is in our bones. When we enter the kingdom battle together with others, we draw close to them.

No more is this experienced than within the context of marriage. The story of Corey and Sarah in chapter ten is a living example of this powerful truth.

But if we're going to fully understand why fighting together draws us together and how it all works, we need to go back to the beginning – the very beginning.

You already know from chapter five that the story of marriage did not start in a garden; it began in heaven when God threw Satan down to earth and then put Adam in the same place. The earth became the scene for an epic showdown between God's arch-enemy and His image bearers.

But we need to look even deeper if we want to fully grasp what's going on in the story of marriage and how we fit into this story of battle.

To do that, we're going to look at two processes – the process for how God created the earth and the process for how He created mankind. The similarities are striking and reveal powerful truths that will help you understand why Satan hates your connection with your marriage partner and why he will stop at nothing to break it up.

To set the foundation, Genesis 1:1-2 tells us, In the beginning, the earth was ...

- Formless
- Void
- Dark

God created the earth, but nothing was on it. It was simply a massive expanse of water that was covered with darkness. And who is the father of darkness? Satan. Fresh off his divine butt-kicking, Satan was roaming the earth.

The rest of Genesis 1 shows us the three-step process in which God prepared the earth for Adam's arrival. Notice the progression:

"And God said, 'Let there be light'" (Genesis 1:3).

- Step One – ILLUMINATION

God had to bring light into the darkness.
"God saw that the light was good, and He separated the light from the darkness" (Genesis 1:4-10).

- Step Two – SEPARATION

God lit it up before He split it up. He separated light from dark, water from sky, and land from water.
"Then God said, 'Let the land produce vegetation; seed-bearing plants' ... let the water teem with living creatures ... let the land produce living creatures ... let us make man in our own image'" (Genesis 1:11-31).

- Step Three – HABITATION

Illumination and separation created the environment for habitation – a place where life could exist. God created plants, fish, animals, and people – all living organisms with seed for reproduction.
God always fills what He forms. He formed the earth, then filled it with life.
Now, this is where it gets really fun, because the very same process God used to create the earth, He used to create mankind. The second chapter of Genesis gives us the details.
"So the man gave names to all the livestock, the birds in the sky and all the wild animals. But for Adam no suitable helper was found" (Genesis 2:20, emphasis added).

STEP ONE - ILLUMINATION

If something "wasn't found," what does that imply? Adam was looking! He had to first be illuminated to his need for a companion before God provided one.

Isn't it interesting that God was not all that Adam needed? The Bible is clear about this.

God + Adam = not good.

God + Adam + Eve = good.

We'll see why this is the case in a moment. Let's jump back into Scripture for step two.

"So the Lord God caused the man to fall into a deep sleep; and while he was sleeping, he took one of the man's ribs and then closed up the place with flesh" (Genesis 2:21).

STEP TWO – SEPARATION

God did not create Eve from dust like He had done with Adam. Why? Because Eve was already within him.

When God created Adam, He created mankind – which included both the masculine and feminine aspects of humanity. But they existed inside one human body. When God performed this divine surgery, He removed feminine from masculine so mankind would be in two human bodies.

One male and one female, with their unique differences and characteristics, is the framework for mankind that reflects the image of God.

Interestingly, before Eve came into the picture, the Hebrew term for Adam is "Aw-Dahm," which means mankind. After Eve was created, the Hebrew term for Adam is simply "Adam," this man.[32]

He was mankind before Eve, the embodiment of both male and female. But he was a specific man after Eve, as he was then the embodiment of a male only.

But the story isn't over. There's one more pivotal step to the process.

"Then the Lord God ... brought her to the man ... That is why a man leaves his father and mother and is united to his wife, and they become one flesh" (Genesis 2:22-25).

STEP THREE – HABITATION

This is a fascinating third step. What God had just separated, He now gives the command to come back together "as one." Why would He do something like that? Well, we believe that God separated what was once one so they could become one by choice.

When God created Eve, He didn't just create a woman; he created a *relationship* between a man and a woman. And when the two choose to come together as one in relationship under God, they fully reflect His image!

Before Eve, God already had a relationship with Adam. But only two parties were involved – God and Adam. In order for mankind to reflect the perfect image of God, which includes three people – Father, Son, Holy Spirit – three parties had to be involved: Adam, Eve, and God.

Can you see now why Satan hates your relationship and wants to rip it apart?

Your marriage reflects the image of his arch-rival, God. When you accept each other as God's gift to one another, just like Adam and Eve accepted each other, you become one and fully reflect His image.

And when you are united together as one, you become the church (Matthew 18:20). And the gates of hell will not prevail against the church (Matthew 16:18). Not only does your marriage reflect God's image, it's also a powerful force against evil.

1. Illumination
2. Separation
3. Habitation

Light always comes first. If you want your marriage to be powerful against Satan and his attacks, then you need God as the central figure in your relationship.

Separation comes next. You embrace each other as unique

and different, both playing important roles in God's plan to subdue Satan.

Finally, habitation. Your ability to experience thriving life within your marriage only comes when you're illuminated to your need for one another, and you fully accept each other as distinct and equally significant.

God used the same three-step process in creating mankind as He used in forming the earth. Isn't that incredible?

But there's another marriage secret buried in Scripture that I want to share with you. It's specific to women and their role as "helper" to their husbands. This truth helped me see Tori in a new way and has strengthened our relationship immensely.

If you're a woman reading this, please tell your husband to get his rear in gear and read this part for himself!

THE HELPER

When God provided Eve, He referred to her as a "helper suitable" for Adam (Genesis 2:20). But she wasn't simply an assistant for the job of ruling the garden; there were plenty of animals to help with that.

What Adam needed was someone that would fulfill a much more important role.

To discover what this role is, we have to go back and look at the original Hebrew meaning of the term "helper suitable." Obviously, I'm not smart enough to know Hebrew words on my own. I got an 820 on my SAT! But I do know how to read, so I thank Skip Moen for the insights in his book, *Guardian Angel,* which helped me better understand the value of my bride.

The Hebrew word for "helper" is 'ezer. It carries several meanings; among them is "first cut from a person" and "first weapon (of defense) of the person." God's word choice to describe the woman indicates she is man's first line of defense, an equal partner equipped with a special function to help him in the fight against their common enemy.[33]

God's plan to fortify Adam against the looming attack of Satan was Eve as the helper. Without her, he was unequipped for the fight.

But here's where it gets crazy: the same word God uses to describe Eve as helper is the same word He uses to describe Himself seventeen times in Scripture! And in about half of those occurrences, it is used to characterize God's relationship to Israel.[34]

David, king of Israel, used this word when he described God in Psalms 46:1, stating, "God is our refuge and strength; a very present *help* in time of trouble" (emphasis added).

For Eve to be the helper was for her to play the same role with her man as God played with Israel. She was to help him in time of trouble. In the context of the garden, this meant trouble had to be brewing. Satan was planning an attack, so God was fortifying against it; He gave Adam the helper he needed to fight and win the battle.

Let me ask a candid question for the husband reading this book right now. If you're in a tough spot where you have to ask for help and someone comes along to help you, who's in the position of strength at that moment?

The helper, right? How foolish would you be to not accept that help?

God is our ever-present help in time of need. But He often meets that need through our wives. He put the helper facet of His nature inside your wife so she can help you when you need it.

It doesn't matter what the problem or trouble is. She can help you! You just need to open up and let her do it.

Having lived through this with Tori, and in counseling plenty of couples, I've discovered that a woman's unique ability to help often manifests itself in her capacity to sense.

God made women to be *sensors* and men to be *solvers*. Women pick up a scent and move toward it, and when they discover what it is, men can often come in and fix it.

I've seen this play out in my business time and time again.

The helper-nature of Tori can sniff things out long before I ever know what's going on. The problem is, she doesn't always know what she's sensing. She just knows "something" is up. If I pay attention to what she's sensing and I wait until she gets clarity, it always pays off for me. But if I don't, it ends up in lost money and lots of frustration.

Trust me. I have the scars to prove it. In all those situations where a business deal went south, I should have let Tori's ability to sniff a problem be a red flag that caused me to stop and wait.

But Eve's role went even further than just a helper. She was a helper suitable. Some translations say "help-meet."

The Hebrew phrase for "helper suitable" is 'ezer kenegdo, which literally means "help-opposite." It's an odd phrase, and this is the only time in Scripture it is used. Eve brings the tension necessary to not only help Adam but also keep him accountable. She is the perfect helper when he obeys God and the perfect "enemy" if he doesn't.[35]

If you're a husband, you're giving a hearty "Amen" to that one, right?

Here's the key: without this tension, there is no power. It would be like stringing up only one side of a bow and arrow. The tension has to be there if you want the arrows to fly.

God has placed us in the context of battle – a spiritual strug-gle that we are meant to fight and win. But we can't do it alone. We need each other. We need the tension that only a divinely constructed counterpart can bring. This is why two people of the same sex do not reflect the image of God in marriage; they were never created with that ability to bring the proper tension necessary to win the battle.

Psalms 127:4 goes even further when it says, "Like arrows in the hand of a warrior, so are the children of one's youth." As a married couple, you are the bow, and your kids are the arrows.

The story of this world began with a man and a woman and a wedding. The story will find its happy ending (a.k.a. new beginning) with Christ and his bride and a marriage feast like nothing anyone has ever seen.

Between those bookends is where we stand. Most of us exchanged our marriage vows without realizing the depth of what those vows meant or the story they are reflecting. Nor did we recognize the spiritual battle we were getting into. But now we know.

Your marriage, and family, were created for war.

You and your spouse might just be at the beginning of your marriage story. Or you may be years into it. But if this is the first time you've come to recognize what an important union your marriage represents, I encourage you to embrace this new perspective.

Why? Because God designed your marriage to be a part of His battle plan against Satan. He made you and your spouse to be divine butt-kickers! And when you operate "as one" under God, you can't lose. Fighting together will draw you together.

Right now, Jesus is in heaven seated at the right-hand of God, and He's waiting on Satan to be made a footstool under His feet (Psalms 110:1). How is that going to happen? Through you, your spouse, your family, and the collective community of believers united together kicking Satan's tail until he's in that posture of surrender. Of course, it hasn't fully happened yet. But it's coming.

Until then, we live in the space between the bookends of the story. Now get out there and fight!

JOIN US ON THE JOURNEY

If you've enjoyed reading about our journey together through *Beauty in Battle*, let's keep the conversation going! We love talking about relationships and coaching couples to overcome obstacles and crush it in their marriages. We talk a lot about the power of emotional intelligence to help you get along and communicate, the proper use of the enneagram to help you understand each other's deep rooted motives and actions more clearly, and how a foundation on solid, Biblical principles are the secret sauce to winning in marriage.

You can tune into our podcast, take one of our online classes or challenges, or even join us at one of our marriage seminars or retreats. Following us on social platforms @JasonAndTori is a surefire way to make sure you're up to date on what we have going on. You can also visit us at JasonAndTori.com.

Wherever you're at in your marriage, just know we seek to be another resource at your disposal and are championing the success of you and your spouse every step of the way!

Jason and Tori

ENDNOTES

CHAPTER 2: A NEW PAIR OF GLASSES

1 Recounted in Stephen Covey's book The Seven Habits of Highly Effective People

CHAPTER 3: A VISION OF US

2 https://renewingallthings.com/spiritual-health/your-brain-and-body-become-what-you-visualize/

3 Travis Bradberry, *Emotional Intelligence 2.0* (TalentSmart, 2009).

4 Chris Fox, *5,000 Words Per Hour* (Chris Fox, 2015).

5 https://medium.com/desk-of-van-schneider/if-you-want-it-you-might-get-it-the-reticular-activating-system-explained-761b6ac14e53

6 Chris Fox, *5,000 Words Per Hour* (Chris Fox, 2015).

CHAPTER 4: LEAVE THE SUITCASE

7 Gary Thomas discusses this concept in his book *Sacred Marriage* (Zondervan, 2015).

8 Gary Thomas, *Sacred Marriage* (Zondervan, 2015).

9   In their book *Boundaries in Marriage,* Drs. Henry Cloud and John Townsend extensively discuss this topic. They're the ones who opened our eyes to these two key components of conflict.

10 Drs. Henry Cloud and John Townsend, *Boundaries in Marriage* (Zondervan, 2002).

CHAPTER 6: I'M TRIGGERED

11 Dr. Caroline Leaf, Switch on Your Brain: The Key to Peak Happiness, Thinking, and Health (Baker Books, 2013).

12 Dr. John Gottman, The Seven Principles for Making Marriage Work (Harmony, 2015).

CHAPTER 7: CANDLELIGHT CHAOS

13 Tim Keller, *The Meaning of Marriage* (Penguin, 2011).

14 Dictionary.com

CHAPTER 8: PUSH IN THOSE DRAWERS

15 Dictonary.com

16 Dr. Caroline Leaf, Switch on Your Brain: The Key to Peak Happiness, Thinking, and Health (Baker Books, 2013).

CHAPTER 10: FIGHTING AS ONE

17 David Mamet, Masterclass, April 20, 2017.

18 Tim Keller, *The Meaning of Marriage* (Penguin, 2011).

19 Tim Keller, *The Meaning of Marriage* (Penguin, 2011).

CHAPTER 11: LET'S MIX IT UP

20 Rick Warren, The Purpose Driven Life (Zondervan, 2012).

21 We thank John and Stasi Eldredge for their book Love and War (WaterBrook, 2009), which helped us understand Satan's accusatory nature.

22   Our good friend and filmmaker Alex Kendrick gave us the original idea of the three D's.

CHAPTER 12: BONEHEAD BASKETBALL

23   Dictionary.com

CHAPTER 13: LIVING THE DREAM

24   Dr. John Gottman, *The Seven Principles for Making Marriage Work* (Harmony Books, 1999, 2015).

CHAPTER 14: THANK YOU, MA'AM

25   Dr. Caroline Leaf is one of the clearest voices today explaining the brain-body connection.

26   Dr. John Gottman, *The Seven Principles for Making Marriage Work* (Harmony Books, 1999, 2015).

CHAPTER 15: LET IT COUNT

27   Bill Johnson, senior leader of Bethel Church in Redding, California.

CHAPTER 16: LET'S HAVE A FOURTH

28   Dr. John Gottman, *The Seven Principles for Making Marriage Work* (Harmony Books, 1999, 2015).

CHAPTER 19: BATTLE *BUDDY*

29   Dr. John Gottman, *The Seven Principles for Making Marriage Work* (Harmony Books, 1999, 2015).

30   Dr. Carolyn Leaf, Switch on Your Brain: The Key to Peak Happiness, Thinking, and Health (Baker Books, 2013).

CHAPTER 21: GO GET 'EM

31   Skip Moen, *Today's Word* (15 Aug. 2018).

APPENDIX B: IN THE BEGINNING

32   Attribution to Jim Garlow, Well Versed.
33   Skip Moen, Guardian Angel, pg. 56.
34   Skip Moen, Guardian Angel, pg. 56.
35   Skip Moen, Guardian Angel, pg. 60.

Made in the USA
Columbia, SC
29 June 2022

62495523R00140